WHO AND WHEN?

IMPRESSIONISM and POSTIMPRESSIONISM

Artists, Writers, and Composers

D1266781

WHO AND WHEN?

IMPRESSIONISM
and
POSTIMPRESSIONISM

Artists, Writers, and Composers

Edited by Sarah Halliwell

RSVP

RAINTREE STECK-VAUGHN
P U B L I S H E R S
The Steck-Vaughn Company

Austin, Texas

Steck-Vaughn Company

First published 1998 by Raintree Steck-Vaughn Publishers,
an imprint of Steck-Vaughn Company.
Copyright © 1998 Marshall Cavendish Limited.

Library of Congress Cataloging-in-Publication Data
Impressionism and postimpressionism: artists, writers, composers/edited by Sarah Halliwell
p. cm. -- (Who and When: v. 6)
Includes bibliographical references and index.
Summary: Discusses the characteristics of the Impressionist and Postimpressionist movements
of the latter half of the nineteenth century and presents some of the major artists, writers, and
composers that flourished in that period.
ISBN 0-8172-4730-0
1. Impressionism (Art) -- Juvenile literature. 2. Postimpressionism (Art) -- Juvenile literature.
3. Arts, Modern -- 19th century -- Juvenile literature. 4. Artists -- Biography -- Juvenile literature.
[1. Impressionism (Art). 2. Postimpressionism (Art). 3. Arts, Modern -- 19th century. 4. Artists.
5. Authors. 6. Composers.] I. Halliwell, Sarah. II. Series.
NX454.5.I4I46 1998
700'.9'034--dc21
97-11619
CIP
AC

Printed and bound in Italy
1 2 3 4 5 6 7 8 9 0 LE 02 01 00 99 98 97

Marshall Cavendish Limited
Managing Editor: Ellen Dupont
Project Editor: Sarah Halliwell
Senior Editor: Andrew Brown
Senior Designer: Richard Newport
Designer: Richard Shiner
Picture administrator: Vimu Patel
Production: Craig Chubb
Index: Ella J. Skene

Raintree Steck-Vaughn
Publishing Director: Walter Kossmann
Project Manager: Joyce Spicer
Editor: Shirley Shalit

Consultants:
Anthea Peppin, National Gallery, London;
Dr. Andrew Hadfield, University of Wales;
Jonathan Kulp, University of Texas.

Contributors:
Andrew Brown, Lorien Kite, Iain Zaczek.

CONTENTS

INTRODUCTION

Impressionism and Postimpressionism were important artistic movements that flourished in the closing years of the 19th century. The main developments took place in France. In the mid-19th century, the French capital, Paris, was the undisputed center of the art world. Artists faced a strict and conservative system, however. To gain success, an artist's work had to win approval at an annual exhibit called the Salon. The Salon juries liked a certain kind of art—art that portrayed an uplifting theme, preferably historical or mythological, painted in a precise and detailed way. And they frowned upon pictures of modern or ordinary subjects.

One group of artists rejected these ideas. Painters such as Camille Pissarro and Claude Monet (*see pages 8 and 38*) wanted to paint pictures that had a direct bearing on people's lives. And they wanted to produce them in a fresh and lively, less formal style. So, instead of exhibiting their work at the official Salon, they mounted their own shows. Between 1874 and 1886, they staged eight exhibits. After the first of these, the group gained its name—the Impressionists.

The Impressionists' favorite subject was Paris itself, a city which had suffered mixed fortunes. It had been occupied by German troops during France's defeat in the Franco-Prussian War (1870 to 1871) and had witnessed further violence during the uprising of a radical regime called the Commune in 1871. At the same time, Paris was undeniably beautiful. The great building program of the 1850s and 1860s had resulted in wide, airy boulevards and spacious parks. And the World Fair of 1889 brought with it the city's most striking landmark, the Eiffel Tower.

The Impressionists celebrated this modernity. They painted the steam-filled chambers of the railroad stations, the liveliest bars and dance halls, and the popular riverside picnic spots. Critics mocked the Impressionists for choosing such "sordid" subjects. Reviewers of Émile Zola's (*see page 80*) emphatically modern novels, with their uncompromising and brutally realistic portraits of 19th-century everyday life, echoed this hostile reaction.

The techniques of the Impressionists provoked even more outrage. They rejected the highly finished paintings which were popular at the Salon. With the recent advances in photography—which had been invented in the 1830s—such attention to detail seemed pointless. A camera could do the job just as well. The artists also dismissed the balanced, well-ordered approach to composition that art schools had been teaching for centuries. A painting, they argued, should not be constructed carefully in a studio. It should be taken directly from nature.

A basic principle of Impressionism, therefore, was painting out-of-doors. Artists like Monet and Pissarro remained true to this approach for most of their careers, while others, such as Édouard Manet and Edgar Degas (*see pages 14 and 20*), tended to work in the studio. Painting directly from nature, the Impressionists were particularly dedicated to portraying subtle changes in light or atmosphere. They enjoyed the challenge of capturing a reflection rippling across the surface of a river, a ray of sunlight peeping through the clouds, or a gust of wind shaking the leaves on a tree. In a similar way, the French composer Claude Debussy (*see page 86*) tried to conjure up an image of the lapping waves of the sea through his music.

This approach to painting meant that the artist had to work very quickly, in order to capture the desired effect before the sun went behind a cloud, or it started to rain. There was no time to mix colors carefully or to portray objects in great detail. Instead, Impressionist artists tended to use short, deft brushstrokes. Some critics of the time saw this new way of painting as sketchiness, and attacked it. Yet this technique created the flickering sense of movement that makes the Impressionist paintings so freshly spontaneous, and brings them alive.

The term Postimpressionism refers to a group of artists who experimented with Impressionism, but found it too restricting. These painters did not work in a single, common style. Each one adapted Impressionist ideas to meet his own needs. Both Paul Cézanne and Georges Seurat (*see pages 32 and 68*) disliked the older artists' emphasis on fleeting effects, and tried to create images of nature that were more solid and lasting. Paul Gauguin and Vincent van Gogh (*see pages 56 and 62*) used Impressionist methods to suggest moods, emotions, or ideas. This was in contrast to the Impressionists, who held the visible world to be art's only subject. The impact of both Impressionism and Postimpressionism was not limited to France, but resounded throughout Europe and the United States—in the work of artists like James Whistler (*see page 26*)—and helped to lay the foundations of modern art.

CAMILLE PISSARRO

Born a decade before Monet, Renoir, and Sisley, Pissarro was the father figure of the Impressionist group. Devoted to painting all his life, he was a vital organizer, teacher, and inspiration for many younger artists.

Camille Pissarro was born on July 10, 1830, on St. Thomas, a Danish colony in the Caribbean. His father, Frédéric, was a Jewish storekeeper who had emigrated to St. Thomas from Bordeaux, in western France. His mother, Rachel, who was also Jewish, was native to the island. She was a widow, with two daughters from her previous marriage.

As soon as Camille was old enough, he went to a small private school on St. Thomas, where he showed an interest in drawing and painting. His father was not pleased about this; he thought art was a waste of time.

LEARNING ART

In 1842, Frédéric decided to send his son to a school in France to continue his education. He instructed the headmaster, Monsieur Savary, to prevent the boy from drawing. Savary, however, was a great lover of art and he ignored the instruction. Instead, he gave Camille art lessons.

Pissarro stayed in France until 1847, when he returned to St. Thomas. His father insisted he enter the family business. But this made Camille very unhappy. One of his duties was to go to the harbor to check the deliveries for the store. Instead, he spent his time sketching the activity of the port.

A GENEROUS TEACHER

One day, when Pissarro was sketching in the harbor, he met a Danish artist called Fritz Melbye. Melbye admired Pissarro's drawings, and they soon became friends. Melbye, who was four years older than Pissarro, taught his new pupil everything he knew, especially how to paint the effects of light.

In 1852, Melbye suggested that they should both go to Venezuela, where he knew a group of writers, poets, and artists. Despite his father's opposition,

Self-portrait, 1873, by Camille Pissarro
The 43-year-old artist painted this subtle and somber portrait of himself a year before the first Impressionist exhibit.

Pissarro decided to leave St. Thomas, and in November, the two artists arrived in Caracas, the Venezuelan capital.

Life in Venezuela was a revelation to Pissarro. He quickly became part of Melbye's circle of friends, taking part in their passionate discussions on art and philosophy. He often made trips to the Orinoco River basin to paint the sunlight and exotic colors of the jungle.

In 1854, Pissarro returned to St. Thomas. He spent a year painting and developing his own, unconventional style. But he found life on the island unbearable. He hated the island's old-fashioned ways. The treatment of slaves on St. Thomas awakened Pissarro's interest in politics, and he became a strong supporter of individual rights. In the fall of 1855, he set sail for France, never to return.

AIMING FOR REALISM

Upon his arrival in Paris, Pissarro enrolled at the prestigious School of Fine Arts. But he did not enjoy it, and thought that its teaching was out-of-date. The school favored imaginative painting, in which the artist aimed to express his emotions, or to tell a story. Pissarro preferred the work of realist painters such as Gustave Courbet, Jean-Baptiste Camille Corot, and Jean-François Millet. These artists aimed instead to depict nature or life in as realistic a way as possible.

The main route to success for young artists of the time was to have their pictures exhibited at the Salon—an annual exhibit held in Paris. In 1859, the Salon accepted one of Pissarro's land-

THE IMPRESSIONISTS

After months of planning and discussion, the Impressionists held their first exhibit in 1874.

Pissarro was one of a group of artists who shared similar ideas. They would meet in cafés and bars to discuss their beliefs (*right*). For some time, they had been planning an alternative to the annual Salon exhibit. They believed that in order for their work to be properly appreciated, it should have its own exhibit.

The group's first exhibit took place in 1874. Nadar, a photographer, donated his studio as a location for the exhibit, and it opened on April 18. But the exhibit was a huge disappointment for the artists involved. The press criticized the paintings, and the public sneered.

scapes. In subsequent years, however, the judges tended to reject his work. He was not alone in this—many other artists who rejected a traditional way of painting also found that they could not exhibit their work.

In 1860, Pissarro met his future wife, Julie Velay. She was a servant girl for the Pissarro family, who were now living in France. Occasionally, she

The group did gain one thing from the show, however—a name for their movement. A journalist seized on the title of one of Claude Monet's paintings, *Impression: Sunrise*, and titled his mocking review, "The Exhibit of the Impressionists."

The critic intended the name "Impressionist" as a term of abuse. It implied that these artists could only paint rough, vague impressions of things, rather than accurate representations of them. But it became a compliment rather than an insult, once artists such as Monet and Pissarro became highly successful.

special exhibit of all the rejected paintings—the Salon des Refusés. Pissarro's work was exhibited alongside the work of Edgar Degas, Claude Monet, and Pierre-Auguste Renoir (*see pages 20, 38, and 44*).

IDEAS ABOUT ART

These artists had much in common, and they soon began to think of themselves as a group. Over the next few years, they would meet in cafés and bars to discuss their ideas about art. Like Corot and Courbet, they thought that they should paint everyday life as realistically as

> "Happy are those who see beautiful things in modest surroundings or where other men see nothing."
> (Camille Pissarro)

possible, rejecting the imaginative and historical art favored by the Salon. They were also influenced by the Japanese art of the day, which used a lighter combination of colors than was usual in European painting. And everyone except Degas agreed with Pissarro that, in order to depict nature accurately, a painter should work outside.

would model for Camille, and soon the two began a love affair. She went to live with the young painter, even though Pissarro's parents disapproved. In 1863, they had a son, Lucien, who would also grow up to become a painter.

In the same year, there was such an outcry at the amount of work turned down by the Salon judges that Napoleon III, the French emperor, ordered a

At this time, Pissarro was having problems earning enough money to

The Boulevard Montmartre, 1897, by Camille Pissarro
Pissarro's evocative painting shows carriages parked along a fashionable Paris street. The bright colors and spontaneous style brilliantly capture the feel of a rainy night.

support his ever-expanding family. At one point, he was forced to take a job painting blinds and shop signs in order to make ends meet.

In 1870, the Franco-Prussian War forced Pissarro to flee to England. He enjoyed living there, especially as he was accompanied by Monet, who had become a great friend and was probably now the strongest influence on his work. The two of them had the opportunity to study English artists, such as John Constable, who they felt had a freer approach to painting than the French.

On returning to France, Pissarro found that Prussian soldiers had wrecked his home. Out of 1,500 paintings, which represented 20 years' work, just 40 survived. Devastated, the artist moved to Pontoise, a small town outside Paris, and began a series of Impressionist paintings. He was joined by his friend Paul Cézanne (*see page 32*), who stayed for two years. The two artists influenced each other's painting, and in 1904, Cézanne would describe himself as "the pupil of Pissarro."

In 1874, Pissarro helped organize, and took part in, the first Impressionist exhibit, which was a disaster. The Impressionist artists were criticized from all sides. In the next 12 years, there would be seven more Impressionist exhibits. Pissarro was the only artist to be represented at every one.

Despite financial hardship and personal tragedy—two of his children died—Pissarro painted some of his finest work during the late 1870s. His exquisite, subtle use of light and shadow prompted one contemporary

> "He was such a
> teacher, he could
> have taught a stone
> to draw correctly."
> (Mary Cassatt)

critic to describe him as "the truest of the Impressionists."

After 1880, Pissarro's style changed radically. He started to concentrate less on landscapes and more on people. He was influenced by Georges Seurat's (*see page 68*) pointillist technique of using tiny dots to reproduce the effects of light. But this style was too rigid and disciplined for Pissarro, and he never really mastered it. Furthermore, Pointillism was unpopular with buyers, and by about 1889, he had abandoned it.

Before long, he had reverted to his old style. He had a solo exhibit in 1892. By now, Impressionism was popular with the general public, and the show was a financial success. At last,

Pissarro—now in his 60s—was able to make a reasonable living from his art.

Late in life, Pissarro became increasingly involved in politics. Since his youth he had been an anarchist—someone who believes that all government should be abolished.

FAILING HEALTH

After a successful exhibit in 1896, Pissarro's main problem was meeting the demand for his work. But by now, his health was failing him. An eye disease forced him to stay indoors, painting what he saw from his windows. Despite this, he produced some of his best work in the last years of his life, traveling around France in order to vary his subject matter.

Pissarro died in November 1903, at the age of 73. He was remembered not only for his talent as a painter but also for his patience and skill as a teacher, and for his kindness and wisdom. He was a much respected father figure to the younger Impressionists.

MAJOR WORKS

1868	PONTOISE
1871	THE ROAD TO ROCQUENCOURT, LOUVECIENNES
1877	RED ROOFS
1888	ÎLE LACROIX, ROUEN
1893	FEBRUARY SUN OVER BAZINCOURT
1901	VIEW OF THE SEINE

ÉDOUARD MANET

One of the most original and influential painters of the 19th century, Manet painted bold scenes from modern life with a new dynamism. Yet, to his dismay, his work met savage criticism throughout his lifetime.

Édouard Manet was born in Paris on January 23, 1832. His father, Auguste, was a wealthy bureaucrat, while his mother, Eugénie, was artistic and musical. Édouard was bored at school. He preferred to stay at home with his mother, who arranged for him and his two brothers to have piano lessons. In the evenings, the boy's uncle taught him to draw.

JOINING THE NAVY

When he was 16, Manet and his father argued over his future career. The young man was determined to be a painter, but Auguste insisted he should go to law school.

Finally, as a compromise, Manet joined the navy. On December 9, 1848, he set sail for Rio de Janeiro, Brazil. But as soon as he returned to France, he begged his father to let him become an artist. Auguste finally agreed. In January 1850, Manet joined the Paris studio of a respected figure painter called Thomas Couture.

Despite his enthusiasm for learning art, the 18-year-old found his master's traditional method of teaching dull and uninspiring. Manet wanted to see the world and to paint it. Once, when he was given a cast of an antique statue to copy, Manet turned it upside down, saying it was "more interesting" that way up.

A SECRET LOVE

In 1850, the young student fell in love with a Dutch piano teacher called Suzanne Leenhoff, and two years later, they had a son. Manet could not tell his father, who would have disapproved. His mother helped him to rent a room for Suzanne and the baby, but Manet kept his family a secret from his father for the next 13 years.

In 1853, Manet traveled to the great art centers of Italy—Venice, Florence,

Studio in the Batignolles Quarter (detail), 1870, by Henri Fantin-Latour
Édouard Manet, the leader of a new, anti-establishment school of art, at his easel.

and Rome—where he copied the works of the Old Masters, a traditional way of studying art. He also traveled to Germany, Holland, and Austria.

When he returned to Paris, the charming and sociable young painter mixed with the cream of artistic society, meeting the city's most brilliant writers and artists. In particular, he became friends with the poet, Charles Baudelaire; the two remained loyal companions until Baudelaire's death in 1867. Manet was generous to his friends who struggled to earn a living through painting or writing—he was always willing to lend them money.

OFFICIAL REJECTION

In 1859, Manet submitted his first canvas to the Salon, the official art exhibit and the center of the French artistic world. But the Salon jury rejected the painting, *The Absinthe Drinker*, which was named for an alcoholic drink popular with the lower classes.

Manet's work was strikingly different from the paintings people were used to seeing. Most artists of the time painted grand, large-scale scenes of historical or mythological subjects. By contrast, *The Absinthe Drinker* was startlingly modern. It showed a drunken man against a dark, gloomy background. The subject was depressing and, unusually, from the lowest end of society. Manet's style was different, too. He applied the paint in loose brushstrokes, giving his work a new spontaneity.

Manet did not let the Salon rejection stop him. Although he had an unconventional approach to painting, he

A PAINTER OF MODERN LIFE

Elegant and sophisticated, Manet took his inspiration from the exciting and varied life in his native city, Paris.

Manet was a modern painter in both his approach to art and his technique. He took his subjects from everyday Parisian life— people of all classes going about their daily lives.

His work was based on his skill at drawing. He carried notebooks with him everywhere, constantly sketching the bustling life he saw in the boulevards (*above right*) and cafés of Paris. With these sketches, Manet gives the impression of having captured a single moment. His paintings retain this effect of immediacy: They appear to have been painted on the spot rather than in the studio, where the artist did

wanted to succeed in the conventional world of the Salon. But, in 1863, a new painting, *Luncheon on the Grass*, was rejected too. Manet was surprised and hurt by the hostile reaction to his work.

LAUGHING CROWDS

The same year, as a result of artists' complaints about the Salon, Emperor Napoleon III set up the Salon des

most of his work. Manet increased this informal nature of his art by asking his family and friends to pose for him, rather than models.

His technique was also modern. He often struggled to get the exact effects he wanted, even repainting parts of the picture, or destroying the canvas completely. Sometimes, he seems to have been concerned only with how the paint looked on the canvas, rather than in telling a story, or making a specific point. In this way, he stands as one of the founding figures of modern art.

Refusés, or "exhibit of the rejected," where all the works rejected by the Salon's jury would be displayed. Hundreds of people flocked to the show. But they came to laugh and mock the paintings, rather than admire them. And Manet's *Luncheon on the Grass*—showing a nude woman sitting on the grass with clothed men—outraged people more than most.

Even though he craved the acceptance of the official art world, Manet soon became known as the leader of a group of rebel artists. People thought he was making a joke of traditional art and was deliberately aiming to shock.

When the Salon accepted and exhibited Manet's *Olympia* in 1865, an even greater storm broke out. The picture showed a naked woman gazing from the picture, in the style of a

> "You have got to belong to your own period, and paint what you see." (Manet on being "modern")

classical nude. Critics and public alike were angry at what they saw. Not only was the artist challenging society's morals, but he was also sneering at the traditions of art.

NOVEL TECHNIQUE

It was not just his shocking subject matter that upset Manet's audience, but also the way the artist used paint on his canvases. Rather than subtly mixing light and shade like other, more traditional artists, Manet used bold, flat patches of light and dark that flattened the objects in his paintings.

Manet also used a limited range of colors, with black being particularly important. Critics scoffed and the pub-

Boating at Argenteuil, 1874, by Édouard Manet
Although Manet usually worked in the studio, he sometimes painted in the open air like his younger Impressionist colleagues. Even so, this outdoor scene shows his preoccupation with figures, rather than with landscapes.

lic laughed. Manet wrote: "Insults are pouring down on me as thick as rain."

Deeply depressed by the violent reaction to his work, Manet stopped painting for a while and traveled to Spain for a short break. When he returned to Paris, he enjoyed a busy social life, spending time in cafés with artists such as Edgar Degas, James Whistler, and Claude Monet (*see pages 20, 26, and 38*).

When his father died in 1862, Manet was free to marry Suzanne. With his inheritance, he now had plenty of money to live on. But he did not stop painting. He was determined to make the public admire his work.

CONTINUED CRITICISM

When Manet's work was again refused, this time for the Paris World Fair in 1867, he set up his own private exhibit. But this ambitious and expensive idea only brought yet more attacks from critics and the public alike. By now, the artist's nerves were so strained by the years of criticism that he challenged a friend, who had written an insulting article, to a duel. The fight went ahead, but it was quickly stopped, and Manet offered his adversary his boots as a token of friendship.

RECOGNITION AT LAST

In July 1870, Paris was besieged by the Prussians during the Franco-Prussian War, causing great hardship in the city. Manet's health was affected and he had a nervous breakdown. But the following year, his luck suddenly changed. Not only did an art dealer called Paul Durand-Ruel buy some 30 canvases, but his paintings were accepted by the Salon for two years in a row. His future success seemed assured.

Manet was now 40. Nonetheless, he continued to be influenced by younger painters, such as Claude Monet, Pierre-Auguste Renoir (see pages 38 and 44), and Berthe Morisot, his sister-in-law. These artists, known as Impressionists, encouraged Manet to experiment with open-air painting and lighter colors. Yet,

although he supported these artists, he still felt that the right approach was through the official Salon channels. Because of this, he refused to exhibit with them at their first exhibit in 1874.

Throughout the mid-1870s, the critics slowly came to appreciate Manet's work. His work no longer seemed so

> "He was a much greater painter than even we thought." (Edgar Degas, shortly before Manet's death)

shocking or revolutionary. In 1881, the Salon even awarded him a medal, and he was named a Chevalier of the Legion of Honor, France's highest honor. At last he had the official recognition he had longed for. But the artist bitterly claimed that acceptance came "too late to repair 20 years' lack of success."

Manet became ill with a disorder of the nervous system. His left foot was very painful, and he experienced bouts of extreme tiredness. Although he was in great discomfort, he continued to paint, increasingly using pastels, which he found less tiring than oils. Steadily, his condition got worse. In March 1883, his left leg became infected, and had to be amputated the following month. He died on April 30, 1883, in terrible agony, at the age of just 51.

MAJOR WORKS

1862	CONCERT IN THE TUILERIES GARDENS
1863	LUNCHEON ON THE GRASS; OLYMPIA
1867	THE EXECUTION OF MAXIMILIAN
1868	PORTRAIT OF ÉMILE ZOLA
1874	BOATING AT ARGENTEUIL
1882	A BAR AT THE FOLIES-BERGÈRES

EDGAR DEGAS

A shy, private man, Edgar Degas drew his inspiration from everyday scenes of modern Paris and its people. He is best known for his paintings capturing the movement and grace of ballet dancers rehearsing.

Edgar Degas was born in Paris on July 19, 1834. His father, Auguste, was a successful banker, and his mother, Célestine, came from a wealthy family. Edgar was just 13 years old when his mother died in 1847, an event which upset him a great deal.

Degas did well at school, and went on to study law. But instead of concentrating on his studies, he spent most of his time in the Louvre—Paris's main art museum—copying the masterpieces he saw there. In 1853, Degas persuaded his father to let him change careers and become an artist. The family converted one of their rooms into a studio for him.

AN ACADEMIC TRAINING

In 1854, Degas began lessons with a painting teacher called Louis Lamothe. Lamothe had been a pupil of the famous French painter Jean-Auguste-Dominique Ingres, who had worked in a style known as "academic." This was a traditional way of painting based on the art of the past. It was France's official style. Academic painters believed that strong lines were more important in a picture than colors. They also believed that history was the only proper subject for any serious artist.

Like other academic teachers, Lamothe encouraged his students to study the work of the Old Masters, such as Michelangelo and Raphael, and to draw from memory. Degas responded by producing large-scale, traditional paintings of ancient history.

In 1855, Degas met Ingres himself, who was then 75 years old. Ingres told him: "Draw lines, young man, many lines, from memory or from nature." The sensitive Degas followed this advice with enthusiasm. He had always had a passion for drawing, and he naturally preferred to use strong outlines. Throughout his career, Degas drew continually, whether he was

Self-portrait, c.1856, by Edgar Degas
The artist shows himself in a typically serious and intense mood around the age of 22.

sketching a face seen in a café, or laboring for months over a carefully posed nude. Drawing was a way of sharpening his powers of observation, and of preparing for his paintings.

NEW INFLUENCES

By the 1860s, Degas's work was changing. He had become an admirer of Ingres's great rival, Eugène Delacroix, who used vivid color rather than strong lines. In 1862, Degas met Édouard Manet (*see page 14*), one of a group of unconventional artists who were rejecting the traditions of academic painting. Rather than depicting great moments in history, these artists were painting scenes of modern city life.

Under the influence of Manet, Degas turned away from his earlier history subjects and concentrated on everyday scenes. He loved horse racing, for example, and often visited the racetrack to sketch the horses and jockeys. He wandered the streets and cafés of Paris as well, drawing ordinary people going about their business.

BEHIND THE SCENES

Degas was also a frequent visitor to the Paris Opéra, or opera house. There, he would sketch the ballerinas as they rehearsed, waited in the wings, or enjoyed brief moments of glory on stage. He was primarily interested in the informal settings of the rehearsal room. Paintings such as *The Dancing Class* reveal rare behind-the-scenes glimpses of life in the ballet.

To suit these new subjects, Degas developed startling compositions that

DEGAS'S DANCERS

Fascinated by graceful movement, Degas found his perfect subject matter in ballerinas.

Degas produced hundreds of sketches, paintings, and models of ballerinas. He enjoyed the challenge of capturing the energy and movement of dancers, and transforming it into art.

He spent countless hours at the Paris Opéra, studying the dancers at work, and building up a vast stockpile of drawings. Then, he would put his studies together to create his final carefully planned compositions.

In *The Dancing Class* of c.1873-75, for example, every tiny detail is closely observed—from the tired dancer stretching in the far corner, to the girl on the piano, scratching her back.

showed the influence of photography, which had been invented in the 1830s. Degas wanted to capture brief snatches of time, as photographers did. He began to work on smaller canvases, sacrificing small details in favor of bold, eye-catching effects.

Degas experimented with blurred focus, distorted angles, and off-center compositions, placing figures with their

This painting has a bold composition typical of Degas's work. He has cut off the dancer on the far right, which gives the painting the immediacy of a quick snapshot.

The figure to the far left heightens the illusion of depth in the painting (*above*). The figures form a dramatic funnel-like triangle. The angled floorboards, and the accents of red that run through the group, strengthen this impression.

Degas was a serious, obsessive worker and he had no time for love affairs. He once commented that "there is love and there is work, and we have only one heart." He did, however, form a close friendship with a fellow artist, the American, Mary Cassatt (*see page 50*).

A STREAK OF BAD LUCK

In 1870, France went to war with Prussia, which is now part of Germany. Degas was drafted into the army and served his time in the artillery. But in 1871, during the Prussian siege of Paris, Degas's eyesight was somehow damaged. He believed that cold air was to blame. For the rest of his life,

> "He is the man who has best captured, in reproducing modern life, its soul." (writer Edmond de Goncourt)

Degas's sight steadily got worse, and he worked with increasing difficulty.

In 1874, Degas's father died, leaving vast debts. Degas's brother, René, had also borrowed large sums of money, and within two years, the banks ordered both brothers to pay their debts. Degas had to sell his house and art collection.

For the first time, Degas had to earn a living by selling his work, something to which he was not suited. He com-

backs to the viewer, or even cut in half by the edge of the picture. These new methods helped create a sense of spontaneity and immediacy in his works, making them seem like "snapshots" of ordinary life. Yet although these images look casual, almost like sketches, they were all carefully planned. "No art was ever less spontaneous than mine," the artist wrote.

The Dancing Class, c.1873-75, by Edgar Degas
Degas captures the young ballerinas as they take a break from their training routine. Little details help to bring the scene alive, such as the dog that hides behind a dancer's leg.

plained bitterly about having to produce pictures to order. He was such a perfectionist that he often asked his customers to return paintings for improvements. Sometimes, he failed to deliver the paintings altogether.

Meanwhile, Degas had become closely involved with a group of artists that included Claude Monet and Pierre-Auguste Renoir (*see pages 38 and 44*). Degas had a very different style from these artists but, like them, he wanted to make art more modern. In 1874, Degas exhibited in the group's first independent exhibit, after which they became known as the "Impressionists." He would take part in six of the group's seven subsequent exhibits.

DEGAS'S PASTELS

The critical abuse that the exhibit received made Degas more determined than ever to experiment. He began using new techniques and media. He turned toward making prints, and started to work with pastels—sticks molded from a paste of powdered pigment; and distemper, a mixture of pigment and glue or egg.

Pastels suited Degas best because they enabled him to draw and color at the same time, allowing him to create rich textures and well-defined shapes. He would dampen his pastels with steam from a kettle, rub them with his fingers to soften them, and then build up layers of brilliant color by scribbling.

Degas's pastel works often depicted hatmakers, laundresses, and nude bathers. Many people found these pictures of working-class women very shocking; they did not consider such ordinary, humble figures suitable subjects for an artist.

By the 1880s, Degas's sight had gotten much worse. He increasingly turned to pastels, which required less effort than painting with oils. He also began to make wax models of dancers.

Failing eyesight was probably also responsible for Degas's worsening temper and unsociable behavior. He had developed a reputation for being cold,

unapproachable, and argumentative. After one violent exchange with Manet, the two artists both returned paintings that they had given to each other as gifts. Degas became a virtual hermit, rarely emerging from his dusty, dimly lit studio, and allowing few people inside.

He worked as hard as his failing health and eyesight allowed him—drawing, modeling, and retouching the pictures of his youth. He continued working well into his 70s, building up vibrant charcoal outlines and blazes of pastel colors. All detail had long since disappeared from his art, and he now created bold and powerful images of bathing women and nudes.

By 1912, failing health and eyesight had brought Degas's art to a halt. Deprived of his favorite pastime, he took to roaming the streets of Paris, wearing a flowing cape. The newly motorized traffic was a constant danger for Degas, and the old man often had to be helped across the road by police officers. Degas died on September 27, 1917.

MAJOR WORKS

1858-60	THE BELLELLI FAMILY
c.1868-69	THE OPÉRA ORCHESTRA
c.1873-75	THE DANCING CLASS; CARRIAGE AT RACES
1874	TWO DANCERS ON STAGE
1876	ABSINTHE
1884	WOMEN IRONING
1888-92	AFTER THE BATH

JAMES WHISTLER

Although Whistler was not a member of the Impressionist group, his work was related to that of his French contemporaries. Like them, he developed a daringly original style of painting that shocked the public and critics.

James Abbott McNeill Whistler was born in Lowell, Massachusetts, on July 10, 1834. His father, Major George Washington Whistler, resigned from the army to become a civil engineer. In 1843, he took his family to Russia, where he had a position supervising the construction of the czar's, or ruler's, railroad. The family lived in style, and the young Whistler learned French and took drawing lessons.

FINDING A CAREER

On the death of his father from typhoid fever in 1849, Whistler's family returned to America. His mother was very religious. She hoped her son would become a minister, but Whistler disliked the idea. Instead, he entered the U.S. Military Academy at West Point, in 1851. He soon found he didn't like the army either, however. During his three years at West Point, his unruly behavior constantly got him into trouble. He finally flunked out for failing a chemistry exam.

By then, Whistler had decided that he wanted to be a painter. In 1855, he sailed for Paris. The following year, he joined the studio of a Swiss painter, Charles Gleyre. He did not spend much time at Gleyre's studio, however. He preferred the company of a circle of young artists that included Édouard Manet (*see page 14*). Their unconventional lifestyle suited Whistler, who threw himself into the role of wit and dandy. He roamed the streets of Paris, dressed in eccentric clothes: a broad-brimmed straw hat, a monocle, a white suit, and patent-leather shoes.

The discussions with his artist friends in Paris helped Whistler establish his own theories of art. He was not interested in painting likenesses of scenes or objects. For Whistler, art was a visual experience. He was interested in the painted surface of the canvas,

James Abbott McNeill Whistler, c.1870s
This photograph shows the eccentric artist posing in a typically self-conscious and theatrical way.

with harmonies of color, the play of light and shade, and the patterns made by shapes.

Whistler thought of pictures as being in some ways similar to music and he often chose titles based on musical terms. His nighttime river scenes were "nocturnes," his portraits were "symphonies" or "harmonies," and his pictures dominated by black and gray were usually "arrangements."

LIVING IN LONDON

In 1859, Whistler went to live in London, at the house of his brother-in-law. He did not stay for long, as the two men fought constantly. On one occasion, Whistler pushed his host through a plate glass window. He moved out to his own studio, where he started painting what was to be his favorite subject for the rest of his life, the Thames River.

By now, Whistler had established himself as an extraordinary personality and an artist of great originality. In 1860, he received critical acclaim when he exhibited *At the Piano* at the Royal Academy. He now began using a model who became his companion for the next seven years—Joanna Hefferman, known as Jo. She appeared in *Symphony in White, No 1: The White Girl*, painted in 1862, which caused a sensation when shown in Paris.

Despite a tempestuous relationship, Whistler and Jo lived together until 1863, when his mother came to England to live with him. Whistler's mother later became the subject of his famous work, *Arrangement in Gray and Black: Portrait of the Painter's Mother*.

THE RUSKIN TRIAL

In 1877, Whistler had to defend his work in court— against one of the century's most important critics.

In July 1877, the influential English art critic John Ruskin launched an attack on Whistler's painting of about 1874, *Nocturne in Black and Gold: The Falling Rocket* (right).

The work, inspired by a firework display on the Thames River in London, was a dark canvas lit up by flashes and explosions of color. It shows Whistler's concern with color, harmony, and the atmosphere of a painting rather than with merely accurately describing what something looked like.

In a savage article, Ruskin denounced Whistler and the "unfinished" appearance of his

After a visit to Chile in 1866, Whistler briefly resumed his relationship with Jo, after which she disappeared from his life. He became increasingly argumentative and intolerant, venting some of his aggression by taking boxing lessons. At the same time, he began to paint his famous *Nocturnes* and portraits.

In the *Nocturnes*, Whistler reduced the subject matter—boats, warehouses,

Whistler was confident that he had at last fulfilled his genius, even though the *Nocturnes* failed to sell. His portraits were more successful, allowing him to pay off the huge debts he had run up with his extravagant lifestyle. In 1875, his mother left London due to ill health, and Whistler's current mistress, Maud Franklin, moved into the house.

One of Whistler's patrons was Frederick Leyland, a wealthy shipowner. When Leyland asked Whistler's opinion of the decor in his house, the artist suggested a few small changes. But while Leyland was away in the summer of

> "The same color should appear in the picture continually here and there ... in this way the whole will form a harmony." (James Whistler)

work. He accused the painter of "flinging a pot of paint in the face of the public."

In a fury, Whistler sued for libel, but although he won the verdict, he was awarded only one farthing in damages—about one cent. The court case caused great commotion and amusement in the press, but it broke Whistler financially.

1876, Whistler covered the dining room with a design of blue and gold peacocks. On his return, Leyland was furious and paid only half of the artist's fee.

A far worse disaster followed in 1877, with the famous Ruskin trial. The cost of the court case pushed Whistler deeper into debt. In 1879, he petitioned for bankruptcy and left for Venice.

In 1880, he returned to London and put on an exhibit that would restore his

bridges, and even people—to simple patches of color. By leaving out detail, Whistler made the viewer focus on the harmonies of colors and the balance of shapes. Before painting, Whistler carefully mixed his colors, sometimes taking longer getting the tones right than in painting the picture itself. He often diluted his paints so thinly that they would run down the canvas.

reputation. In 1885, he gave his famous "Ten O'Clock Lecture," in which he set out his views on art. Around this time, he also met a woman artist, "Trixie" Godwin, whom he married in 1888.

This was the period of Whistler's greatest success. The city of Glasgow, in Scotland, bought his portrait of the historian Thomas Carlyle for a large sum of money. And the French government bought the portrait of Whistler's mother and made him an officer of the Legion of Honor. A large exhibit of his work in 1892 attracted many collectors.

Whistler and Trixie now moved to France. But Trixie fell ill, and they had to return to London. When she died of cancer in 1896, Whistler was devastated. He was now suffering from a circulatory illness, which made him feel cold all the time. In 1900, he went to North Africa to try to improve his health, but it had little effect. Three years later, weakened by pneumonia and heart disease, Whistler died in London.

MAJOR WORKS

1858-59	AT THE PIANO
1862	SYMPHONY IN WHITE, NO 1: THE WHITE GIRL
1871	ARRANGEMENT IN GRAY AND BLACK: PORTRAIT OF THE PAINTER'S MOTHER
c.1871-74	NOCTURNE: GRAY AND GOLD—WESTMINSTER BRIDGE
c.1874	NOCTURNE IN BLACK AND GOLD: THE FALLING ROCKET

Arrangement in Gray and Black: Portrait of the Painter's Mother, 1871, by James Whistler
Whistler painted his mother while she was staying with him in London in 1871. Whistler
insisted that its primary importance was as an "arrangement" in black and white.

PAUL CÉZANNE

Shunning the art world of Paris in favor of the sunlight of southern France, Paul Cézanne developed a revolutionary style of painting, which established him as the so-called "father of modern art."

Paul Cézanne was born on January 19, 1839, in Aix-en-Provence, a small city in the south of France. His father, Louis-Auguste, ran a hat shop and the city's bank. In 1852, the 13-year-old Cézanne went to Bourbon College in Aix. He was a good student, but made few friends. His closest friend was Émile Zola, who later became a famous writer (*see page 80*).

EARLY DREAMS

At first, Cézanne wanted to be a poet. But his interest shifted to art, and he began attending a local art school. Letters from Zola, who had gone to Paris to study, filled him with dreams of leaving for the capital city to live as an artist. But he lived in fear of his powerful father. Louis-Auguste wanted his son to be a lawyer, and, in 1859, Paul entered law school in Aix.

He had not given up his ambitions of being an artist, however. Upon passing his final examinations, Cézanne told his parents that he was becoming a painter.

They were very unhappy. But they gave him a small allowance and even helped him move to Paris in April 1861.

Six months later, he was back home in Aix. Despite Zola's encouragement, he had failed to meet many other painters in Paris. Before leaving the city, he destroyed all his canvases, convinced that he would never be a successful artist. But in November 1862, after a tedious year working at his father's bank, Cézanne returned to Paris. This time he was determined to make his mark on the art world.

FAILURE

Success did not come easily, though. He failed the entrance test for France's official painting school, the School of Fine Arts. Year after year, he sent his paintings to the Salon, the official state exhibit. But each time, the Salon judges

Self-portrait, c.1880, by Paul Cézanne
Cézanne painted many portraits of himself throughout his life. This one shows the painter in his early forties.

refused to show them. Cézanne's attitude may be partly to blame: He gave his paintings offensive titles, delivered them late, and wrote rude letters to government arts officials.

A DIFFICULT CHARACTER

Cézanne was a very difficult person. He was shy, and hated to be touched. He was filled with self-doubt, yet suspected other artists of stealing his ideas. He was also bad-tempered and quarrelsome. He continually fought intense feelings of anxiety and fear. His early paintings mirrored this inner turmoil—dark, violent images of evil and death. But despite his awkward personality, fellow painters were beginning to notice him. One of the Impressionists, Pierre-Auguste Renoir (*see page 44*), later declared: "From the very start, even before I had seen his painting, I felt he was a genius."

A NEW FAMILY

At the age of 30, Cézanne's life, and the way he painted, suddenly changed. In 1869, he met Hortense Fiquet, and the couple began a relationship. At the same time, he abandoned the darker fantasies of his early work and turned toward painting landscapes, working in the open air, like the Impressionists.

In 1872, Hortense gave birth to a son, also named Paul, whom the artist adored. But Cézanne was still so terrified of his father that he kept the birth a secret for years. In the same year, Cézanne took his new family to Pontoise, a village near Paris, where the artist Camille Pissarro lived (*see page*

BLOCKS OF COLOR

Cézanne's style laid the foundations for the major art movements of the 20th century.

Paul Cézanne was not interested in imitating the real world. Instead, he was concerned with reconstructing three-dimensional shapes and the space between objects without breaking the flatness of the canvas.

Cézanne achieved his aim in various ways. He built up objects with distinct, dashlike blocks of color, overlapping the patches of paint so that one object appeared to be in front of another. He also used the visual effect of warm colors, such as reds and yellows, which seem to jump forward in a painting, to contrast with the effect of cold colors, such as blues and greens,

8). Over the next two years, Cézanne and Pissarro worked side by side. Pissarro showed Cézanne the techniques of Impressionist painting, and ensured that his works were shown at the first Impressionist exhibit in 1874.

Cézanne's time with Pissarro was important for his artistic development. Although he moved beyond Impressionism, he always preferred painting

which recede. Cézanne also showed objects from several viewpoints at once, making them seem to come right out of the painting.

Early in his career, Cézanne used parallel, oblong brush-strokes (*above top*). But later, he began to use more loosely defined, and often squarish patches of color (*above*).

directly from nature, as the Impressionists did. On fine days he would set out in his broad-brimmed hat and heavy boots, with his canvas on his back.

During the next ten years, Cézanne led a solitary, calm existence, dividing his time between Paris and Aix. Quietly, slowly, and carefully, he developed his own unique style of painting. He would work on a picture for months, some-

times years. A dab of color here would be balanced by another there, in a slow, painstaking process.

PAINTING LANDSCAPES

Cézanne was happiest painting landscapes in and around Aix. Some places were of particular importance to him and he would paint them time and time again. He was obsessed with the limestone mountain Mont Sainte Victoire, for example, producing around 60 pictures of it. Ignoring surface detail, he reduced the scene before him to its most fundamental forms, showing it as a mass of basic geometric shapes.

He also painted many still lifes, such as *Apples and Oranges*. Although

> "See in nature the cylinder, the sphere, and the cone."
> (Paul Cézanne)

the objects in the painting seem to be placed in a haphazard fashion, Cézanne would spend hours carefully arranging them so that they were just right.

AN EVENTFUL YEAR

In 1886, three crucial events occurred in Cézanne's life. First, his friend, Émile Zola, published *L'Oeuvre*—or *The Masterpiece*—a novel about a failed artist who commits suicide. Cézanne believed that Zola had modeled the character on him. He was deeply

Mont Sainte Victoire, c.1905, by Paul Cézanne
Cézanne was fascinated by this huge limestone mountain and painted it many times between 1904 and 1906. The canvas is made up of blocks of subtle color.

offended, and never saw the writer again. The second event took place a few weeks later, when Cézanne, who had at last admitted the existence of his secret family, married Hortense. Finally, in October 1886, Cézanne's father died, leaving his son a fortune.

The events of 1886 encouraged the artist to withdraw even more from the world. Hortense and the young Paul

Vollard, organized a one-man show of his work in Paris. It was the first time Cézanne's paintings had been seen in the capital for nearly 20 years. Although the public did not understand his works, his fellow artists recognized the genius of his revolutionary technique.

FINAL YEARS

From then on, admirers from Paris made regular pilgrimages to Aix to see Cézanne, who seems to have enjoyed the attention. In other respects, his old age was uneventful. In 1901, he bought a plot of land on a hill just outside Aix, and had a studio built on the site. Each day, he walked there to work. In later years, as his health got worse, Cézanne traveled by carriage instead of walking. One day, angered at a small increase in the fare, he stubbornly walked to the studio, and got caught in a downpour of rain. As a result of his drenching, he caught pneumonia. A week later, on October 22, 1906, he died.

MAJOR WORKS

1873	HOUSE OF THE HANGED MAN
1877	MADAME CÉZANNE IN A RED ARMCHAIR
1888-90	HARLEQUIN
1890-02	THE CARD PLAYERS
1895-1900	APPLES AND ORANGES
1898-1905	THE BATHERS
c.1905	MONT SAINTE VICTOIRE

stayed in Paris, while Cézanne lived in Aix, visiting his wife and son occasionally. He was so successful in cutting himself off from people in Paris that many forgot about him. Some younger artists even thought that he was dead.

But then in 1895, when Cézanne was 56, the famous art dealer, Ambroise

CLAUDE MONET

The most determined and single-minded of the Impressionist group, Monet aimed to capture nature's fleeting moments. At first, people mocked his work, but he remained dedicated to capturing visual sensation in paint.

Claude-Oscar Monet was born in Paris on November 14, 1840. Five years later, his father took over the family store in Le Havre, on the Normandy coast of France. Monet grew up in the busy port. His aunt was an amateur painter and she encouraged the boy's talent for drawing. By the time he was 15, he had gained a local reputation and had already sold a few paintings.

TRAINING WITH BOUDIN

A successful local landscape painter, Eugène Boudin, saw Monet's drawings on show in a shop. When he met Monet in 1858, he took the young man under his wing. Boudin was a specialist in beach scenes, and liked to paint in the open air. At the time, this was an unusual thing to do. Monet enjoyed painting alongside Boudin. And by the age of 17, he had decided that his vocation in life was to paint landscapes from nature.

Although Monet loved painting the wild Normandy coast, Paris was the artistic center of the world. So, in 1859, he went to the capital to pursue his studies. His father wanted him to study at the official state art academy, the School of Fine Arts, but Monet chose the independent Atelier Suisse school, an open studio where there were no formal lessons or examinations. The decision angered his father, who cut off Monet's allowance.

At the Atelier Suisse, Monet met Camille Pissarro (*see page 8*), who was to become a key figure of the Impressionist group. He also went to bars in Montmartre, a suburb of Paris, where unconventional artists, such as Édouard Manet (*see page 14*), met to discuss art.

Monet's involvement in the cultural life of Paris came to an end, however, when he was drafted into the army. Between 1861 and 1862, he served in Algeria, northwest Africa, but he got

Monet in his floating studio (detail), 1874, by Édouard Manet
Manet captures the artist working in his specially built riverboat at Argenteuil.

sick, and went home to recover. His family paid the army to release him from his military service.

In 1862, Monet returned to Paris to study under Charles Gleyre, a well-known teacher. Monet often found his traditional methods of painting frustrating. Gleyre taught his pupils to paint scenes from history and to study the paintings of Old Masters. Yet he also encouraged them to paint in the open-air, an unusual practice at that time. Gleyre tended to leave Monet and his fellow-student Pierre-Auguste Renoir (*see page 44*) "much to their own devices." Together with other students from the studio, they often went to the forests around Paris, spending hours painting.

IMPRESSIONS OF LIGHT

Monet's aim was to catch the passing impressions of light and atmosphere, the "most fleeting effects," as he called them. He wanted to show what his eye could actually see, rather than what his mind knew was there. To capture these effects, Monet developed a painting technique that enabled him to work quickly. He also used bright, pure colors, rather than the dark tones of traditional artists. Sometimes, he used the handle of his brush to scratch through the paint surface and create a more broken, textured effect.

In 1864, Gleyre was forced to close his studio because of an eye ailment. Monet's family, dismayed at their son's unconventional lifestyle, again cut off his allowance. After this, Monet lived in poverty for a number of years. In 1867, his girlfriend, Camille Doncieux, gave

(*see page 44*)

SERIES PAINTINGS

In his attempt to capture the effects of light, Monet painted the same subjects over and over again.

Monet began working on his series paintings in the late 1880s. He wanted to capture the fast-changing effects of natural sunlight at different times of the day. This meant painting in the open air with a speed and fervor no earlier artist had attempted.

When working on his first major series, *Haystacks*, from around 1890, Monet would carry several unfinished canvases around with him in a wheel-barrow. If the light changed, even slightly, he would quickly switch to another canvas that matched the new conditions. He would then finish the works back in the studio.

birth to a son, but Monet, who was staying near Le Havre at the time, was so poor that he could not afford to travel back to Paris to see them.

In 1870, Monet married Camille. That same year, war broke out between France and Prussia. To avoid being drafted, Monet left France and traveled to England. Camille and their son, Jean, later joined him in London.

Even stormy conditions did not deter him. With water streaming under his cape, he would hold a few canvases between his knees, placing them on his easel one after another, each for a few minutes.

During the 1890s, Monet suffered increasingly from rheumatism, which made working outside difficult. So when painting his *Rouen Cathedral* series, between 1892-95, he rented a studio nearby, so he could paint his huge subject from the window, protected from the elements (*above*).

Monet spent his time studying the work of English landscape artists and painting views of parks and the Thames River. In London, he met the French art dealer Paul Durand-Ruel, who was the first dealer to recognize Monet's importance. His consistent support rescued the artist from poverty.

In 1871, Monet returned to France and rented a house at Argenteuil, a village on the Seine River a few miles outside Paris. This was one of the most fruitful periods in Monet's life: he was happily married and life on the river provided him with many subjects to paint. Renoir and Alfred Sisley, another Impressionist painter, often visited him and the three men would work together.

THE FIRST EXHIBIT

In 1874, Monet and his associates held their first exhibit as a group. The artists on show also included Edgar Degas, Paul Cézanne, Pierre-Auguste Renoir, and Mary Cassatt (*see pages 20, 32, 44, and 50*). The exhibit was a terrible failure. The startling new styles shocked many viewers. Critics said that the bright colors and bold brushwork made the paintings look unfinished. One of Monet's works, *Impression: Sunrise*, prompted a critic to write a sarcastic article called "Exhibit of the Impressionists." The name stuck.

After the exhibit, Monet's debts mounted. In 1878, he moved to Vétheuil, still on the Seine, but farther away from Paris. The following year, Camille died after a long illness. Alice Hoschedé, the wife of a collector of Impressionist paintings, who had nursed Camille, took over the care of Monet's two sons. She also cleared his debts. Over the next few years, Monet moved to various locations along his beloved Normandy coast, tirelessly painting nature as he saw it.

In 1883, Monet bought a house he had once rented in Giverny, a village about 40 miles northwest of Paris. At the same time, he continued to travel in

Impression: Sunrise, 1872, by Claude Monet
This view of Le Havre harbor stunned the public and gave Impressionism its name when it went on show in 1874. "What freedom, what ease of workmanship!" mocked a critic.

search of interesting subjects. Throughout the 1880s, he worked on the Mediterranean coast, as well as in northern France. Meanwhile, the works of Monet and the other Impressionists were at last becoming popular, and were beginning to sell in large numbers, thanks mainly to the efforts of Durand-Ruel. In 1883 alone, the art dealer organized Impressionist exhibits in

showing them at different times of the day. These works were very popular. In 1891, Durand-Ruel organized an exhibit of the haystack paintings. It sold out after only three days.

MONET'S WATER GARDEN

By 1892, Alice Hoschedé's husband had died, and she and Monet were married. He continued to travel, but now he focused more and more on the beautiful, Japanese-style water garden that he had created at Giverny. He had built a pond and filled it with water lilies.

The garden became the center of Monet's artistic life. He painted it again and again. For the last 30 years of his life, the water lilies were virtually his only subject. He painted ever larger pictures of the plants, the largest being 40 feet wide, creating shimmering pools of floating color.

Despite his failing sight, Monet worked right up until his death on December 5, 1926. He was buried in the cemetery of Giverny's small church.

MAJOR WORKS

1872	IMPRESSION: SUNRISE; REGATTA AT ARGENTEUIL
1873	WILD POPPIES
1877	GARE SAINT-LAZARE
c.1890	HAYSTACKS SERIES; POPLARS SERIES
c.1892-95	ROUEN CATHEDRAL SERIES
1899-1926	WATER LILIES SERIES

Germany, England, the Netherlands, and the United States.

Throughout the following decade, Monet concentrated on the most original feature of his later career: his series paintings. In these, he painted the same subjects—haystacks, poplar trees, and Rouen Cathedral—over and over,

PIERRE-AUGUSTE RENOIR

Throughout a long career, Renoir's paintings always remained joyful. He loved to paint women, sunny days, and people enjoying themselves; and his lively, colorful Impressionist style expressed his enthusiasm.

Pierre-Auguste Renoir was born on February 25, 1841, at Limoges in central France. His father, Léonard, was a tailor, and his mother, Marguérite, a seamstress. In 1844, the family moved to Paris where they settled in a run-down apartment.

A TALENTED BOY

Although the family was very poor, and life was difficult, Pierre-Auguste had a happy childhood. He was a great talker and joker, and he made friends very easily. He also had a beautiful singing voice. Charles Gounod, a famous composer, gave the young boy music lessons and offered him a place in the Paris Opéra choir. But even at the age of 13, Renoir felt that a musical career was not for him. Instead, he took up another offer—to become an apprentice painting pictures on porcelain.

He was very skillful at the job. His fellow workers gave him the nickname "Mr. Rubens," for the great 17th-century artist, and his employer suggested that he should train properly as a painter. His parents could not afford the expensive tuition fees, however.

A VITAL INFLUENCE

By 1862, at the age of 21, Renoir himself had saved enough money to enter the studio of Charles Gleyre, a well-known portrait-painter and teacher in Paris. Gleyre mainly taught in a traditional way. Yet he also stressed the importance of painting outdoors, which was not a common practice at that time. Painting outside had a great influence on Renoir and his fellow pupils, who included Claude Monet (*see page 38*), Frédéric Bazille, and Alfred Sisley. They often painted together in the forests outside Paris.

Working outdoors, where they could not control the light as in a studio, the artists had to paint quickly. Otherwise

Pierre-Auguste Renoir, 1865, by Frédéric Bazille
Bazille painted this portrait of his friend when they were both in their early 20s.

they would not be able to capture the colors in nature before they changed. Also, the artists did not have the time to blend their brushstrokes on the canvas in the traditional precise way. Instead, they placed different colors side by side.

Renoir's use of color now changed. Until this time, Renoir had painted much of his work with dark, heavy paints. But, under the influence of his friends, he began to use lighter colors and a more delicate touch.

THE IMPRESSIONISTS

These young, dynamic painters also met with other progressive artists, including Édouard Manet and Edgar Degas (*see pages 14 and 20*), who preferred to paint everyday scenes rather than history. They spent long evenings in Paris cafés, passionately discussing art. Gradually, the ideas that led to Impressionism emerged.

During the late 1860s, Monet and Renoir worked closely together. They were both attracted to sparkling river scenes and views of Paris's bustling street-life. Sometimes, they painted identical scenes, but Renoir's style was softer than Monet's. In 1869, they both painted a restaurant at a spot on the Seine River called *La Grenouillère*—the frog-pond. These two paintings mark the birth of the Impressionist style.

This time was a period of severe financial hardship for Renoir. He often went without food so that he could buy materials. He later said: "I would have given up several times, if Monet had not reassured me with a slap on the back."

PAINTING FOR PLEASURE

For Renoir, painting was a way of expressing his pleasure in life. His works are filled with celebration.

Renoir loved to paint people enjoying themselves. Renoir only painted when he felt happy, and he deliberately chose subjects that he considered attractive: lush landscapes, fruit and flowers, people enjoying themselves, children playing and, above all, beautiful women.

Often, the people having fun were people he knew. In *The Luncheon of the Boating Party*, for example, he captured the relaxed, lazy mood of a group of his friends dining beside the Seine River. The young woman to the left of the picture is Aline Charigot, Renoir's wife-to-be. And to her left is the landlord of

In 1870, however, the collaboration between Renoir and Monet ended when war broke out between France and Prussia, now northern Germany. Renoir spent the war in the south of France, training horses for the cavalry. He returned to Paris after the war ended in 1871, and resumed his painting.

Renoir had developed a fascination with the effect of light passing through

the restaurant, M. Fournaise, and his daughter (*above*).

Although it looks natural and spontaneous, the scene was carefully arranged. A friend of the artist, named Baron Barbier, organized it. He rounded up all Renoir's friends and even made sure the boats were properly positioned for the background. Then, the artist began to make sketches on the spot, to work up later in his studio.

It was one of his most popular works. As one critic commented, "The Impressionists reach the summit of their art when they paint our French Sundays."

was soon selling enough to move into a large studio in Paris. Renoir was popular and his studio became a meeting place for the Impressionists. Throughout the 1870s, he organized Impressionist shows, and exhibited regularly with the group.

DIFFERENT REACTIONS

Renoir's money problems were not over, however. Traditional artists and critics ignored or ridiculed Renoir's work—one critic compared one of his nudes to a "mass of rotting flesh."

The critics and the public had harsh things to say about all the Impressionist painters. But slowly, a small band of

> "I never think that I have finished a painting of a nude, until I feel that I could pinch it." (Renoir)

trees and forming dappled shadows on the ground. In his painting of a Paris dance hall, *Le Moulin de la Galette,* he used bright blues to cover his canvas with such shadows. Renoir visited the scene of the painting every day, immersing himself in its atmosphere and making sketches on the spot.

In 1873, the art dealer Paul Durand-Ruel began to buy his paintings. Renoir

devoted enthusiasts developed. One of them, Victor Choquet, bought a large number of Renoir's paintings. This gave the painter enormous confidence, but it was not enough to support him. He depended on a regular income from producing portraits of wealthy middle-class families. As long as he received these commissions, Renoir could continue with his more experimental, ambitious works.

Luncheon of the Boating Party, 1881, by Pierre-Auguste Renoir
In this vibrant, colorful painting, Renoir shows a merry group of friends lunching on the terrace of a favorite restaurant that overlooked the Seine River.

Up to now, Renoir had remained single. There had been romances, but he saw marriage as a distraction from painting. Around the age of 40, however, he met Aline Charigot, who was some 20 years younger than himself. Aline had modeled for Renoir, but in the summer of 1881, they became much closer. Renoir taught Aline to swim, and they danced and went boating together.

Although the couple loved each other, they had different plans for the future. Aline wanted to start a family in her small, home village in Burgundy, central France. Renoir, on the other hand, was reluctant to leave Paris and did not want children. In late 1881, Aline ended their relationship.

At the same time, Renoir began to distance himself from the rest of the Impressionists, who he felt were becoming too revolutionary in their art. He then began to travel. He went first to northern France, then to Algeria, Spain, and Italy, where he saw the art of the Renaissance painters.

But Renoir could not forget Aline, and in 1882, he returned to Paris to marry her. It was a happy marriage and the couple had three sons. Aline also gave him peace of mind and "time to think," as Renoir later remarked.

Renoir then absorbed all that he had seen on his travels into a dramatically new way of painting. He later told a friend "I had traveled as far as Impressionism could take me and I realized that I could neither paint nor draw."

He developed a "harsh" technique, surrounding his soft, plump figures with hard outlines. He also began to use warmer colors, especially reds. At first, his dealer found this new style of work difficult to sell. After 1885, however, it

> ## "Why shouldn't art be pretty? There are enough unpleasant things in the world." (Renoir)

became more popular, especially in the United States.

Although he was not rich yet, Renoir was now able to move his family to a larger house. The artist was enjoying life. During the week, he worked hard, selling lots of paintings. On Saturday evenings, he would see his friends, and on Sundays he visited his mother.

In 1897, however, disaster struck. Following a cycling accident, Renoir suffered a serious attack of arthritis. Slowly, the disease started to cripple him. Somehow, though, aided by his family, he continued to paint.

To relieve the pain, Renoir spent long periods in the warmth of the French Riviera. In 1907, he built a beautiful house in Cagnes, which became his base for painting. The brilliant light and relaxed atmosphere helped ease his pain, and released a flood of creativity in a new colorful style.

PAINFUL LAST YEARS

But the beauty of the place could not cure the arthritis. By 1912, Renoir's arms and legs were crippled and he was confined to a wheelchair. Nonetheless, he continued to paint right up to his death, pausing only briefly when Aline died in 1915. He also took up sculpture—with two assistants acting as his hands, since his own were too crippled.

In his later years, Renoir had a special glass studio constructed in his garden. Each day, his assistants carried him there in a sedan chair, placed him in his wheelchair, and pushed a paintbrush between his twisted fingers. One day in December 1919, after Renoir had finished painting, he said "I think I am beginning to understand something about this." He died later that night, at the age of 78.

MAJOR WORKS

1869	LA GRENOUILLÈRE
1874	THE THEATER BOX
1876	LA MOULIN DE LA GALETTE
1881	LUNCHEON OF THE BOATING PARTY
c.1881-86	THE UMBRELLAS
c.1888	AFTER THE BATH

MARY CASSATT

Painting at a time when people often did not take women artists seriously, the American Mary Cassatt made her mark working with the Impressionist group in Paris, creating memorable images of the daily life of women.

Mary Cassatt was born on May 22, 1844, in Allegheny city, which is now part of Pittsburgh, Pennsylvania. She came from a wealthy and cultured background. Her father was a successful stockbroker, while her mother was well-educated and spoke fluent French. This proved a useful skill, as the family traveled widely in Europe during Mary's childhood. One of the Cassatts' excursions, to Paris in the 1850s, ended in tragedy, however, with the sudden death of Mary's younger brother, Robbie. After this, the family returned to America.

THE ART STUDENT

In 1861, at the age of 17, Mary enrolled at the Pennsylvania Academy of Fine Arts. This was an ambitious step to take at a time when most young women were expected to settle for a life of marriage and domesticity. Her father was horrified when he heard of her plans, and is reported to have said: "I would almost rather see you dead." His anger must have been even greater when, at the end of her courses, Mary announced that she wished to complete her artistic training in France. Nevertheless, she was allowed to go, and she sailed to Europe in 1866.

In Paris, Mary entered the studio of Charles Chaplin, a mediocre, academic painter—an artist who worked in a traditional way, based on the art of the past. She spent her time studying the Old Masters in the Louvre, the capital's major art gallery. She also studied the work of controversial modern figures such as Édouard Manet (*see page 14*), which she found exciting and inspiring.

Cassatt's own progress was rapid and, in 1868, one of her pictures, *The Mandolin Player*, was accepted at the Salon. This was the most important exhibit in France. An appearance there was the goal of every aspiring artist.

Self-portrait, c.1880, by Mary Cassatt
In this delicately colored watercolor, Cassatt shows herself seated before her work, a traditional artist's pose.

Cassatt did not have the opportunity to build on this promising start right away. Following the outbreak of the Franco-Prussian War in 1870, she moved back to America. She returned to Europe the next year, however, and traveled in Italy, Spain, and Belgium. She did not live in Paris again until 1874, when she resumed her career in earnest. It was to be a momentous year.

THE IMPRESSIONISTS

In April, a revolutionary group of artists called the Impressionists held the first of their eight shows. One of them, Edgar Degas (*see page 20*), became a great admirer of Cassatt's work. Pausing in front of one of her portraits at the Salon, he exclaimed: "It's true, there is somebody else who feels as I do."

Degas did not actually meet Cassatt until 1877, when he visited her studio and suggested that she should exhibit with the Impressionists. His timing was perfect. Cassatt had become bored with academic art, and one of her paintings had just been rejected by the Salon. She immediately accepted Degas's offer. She later told her mother that the opportunity allowed her "to work with absolute independence and without concern for the eventual judgment of a jury .... I hated conventional art. I began to live...." Exhibiting with the Impressionists gave Cassatt an increased sense of confidence, and she produced her best work after 1877.

In common with the other Impressionists, Cassatt preferred to paint scenes from modern, everyday life, rather than subjects from history or

---

JAPANESE INSPIRATION

Like many of the Impressionists, Cassatt was strongly influenced by Japanese color prints.

In 1890, an exhibit of Japanese prints held at the School of Fine Arts in Paris took the French capital by storm. The distinctive use of flat vibrant color, simple shapes, and bold outlines of the prints captivated many artists, including Cassatt.

The American wrote her fellow Impressionist Berthe Morisot in April that year to tell her about the exhibit. She said: "We could go to see the Japanese prints at the School. Seriously, *you must not* miss that. You ... could not dream of anything more beautiful. I dream of it and don't think of anything else except for color on copper ...."

---

mythology. This was not easy, though, since her gender prevented her from portraying many of Impressionism's most popular subjects. As a respectable woman, she could not go to the bars, dance halls, and brothels that her male colleagues painted. Even the portrayal of men presented problems, as social convention made it difficult for her to be alone with a man in her studio.

Cassatt adopted the flat areas of color and the emphasis on decorative patterns typical of Japanese art, bringing a new freshness to her work (*above*).

It was not only the style of Japanese prints that appealed to Cassatt. Many of the works focused on the daily life of women, one of the artist's favorite subjects.

Not surprisingly, therefore, Cassatt concentrated on the daily routines of women. Her subjects ranged from cultural pursuits—such as reading, going to the theater, or playing an instrument—to more domestic activities, such as sewing or drinking tea. Above all, she painted mothers looking after young children—a theme which must have had a certain charm for her, as she

had no children of her own. Despite this, she had no shortage of models. Her mother and sister had moved back to France in 1877 and, three years later, her brother Alexander came over for an extended stay with his four children.

A CLOSE FRIENDSHIP

Cassatt's friendship with Degas lasted until his death in 1917. The precise nature of their relationship is uncertain, as Cassatt burned all their letters in her old age, but they may have been in love. Their artistic links are clearer, however, as many of Cassatt's pictures are similar to Degas's work. In particular, she shared his taste for choosing unusual

> "Our value lies in feeling, in intuition, in our vision that is subtler than that of men."
> (Mary Cassatt)

viewpoints, and for cropping the edges of some figures to make her pictures look like snapshots. Degas even helped Cassatt on one painting, adding some of the background details of her bold and brightly colored painting, *Little Girl in a Blue Armchair*, dating from 1878.

Also like Degas, Cassatt did not work exclusively in oils, but in prints and pastels as well. With these, she produced some of her finest and most original works. Her enthusiasm for

Little Girl in a Blue Armchair, 1878, by Mary Cassatt
This vibrant and bold painting is the only work known to have been a collaboration between Cassatt and her mentor Edgar Degas, who worked on the background.

prints was stimulated by an exhibit of Japanese woodcuts in 1890. Her work in pastel again owed much to Degas. Like him, she adopted a technique that made the colors seem brighter and more intense.

DISAPPOINTMENT

The two artists' association was not always easy, however, as Degas could be moody, and he was often critical of Cassatt. In addition, he had a very low opinion of female painters in general. It was a tribute to Cassatt's strength of character that their friendship endured as long as it did.

A more serious concern, from her point of view, was the way her new,

unconventional artistic direction affected her reputation. She was deeply disappointed, for example, when *Little Girl in a Blue Armchair* was not accepted for the prestigious Universal Exhibit of 1878—especially when she learned that one of the three judges was not even an art critic, but a pharmacist.

The final Impressionist exhibit was staged in 1886; afterward, Cassatt was obliged to branch out on her own. In April 1891, she held her first one-woman show at the gallery of Paul Durand-Ruel, a Paris art dealer who was one of the Impressionists' most loyal and influential supporters.

Then, a year later, she received a prestigious commission to design a mural for the Women's Building at the 1893 World's Fair in Chicago. The theme was to be "Modern Woman." Cassatt had a large trench dug in the floor of her studio so that she could work more easily on the huge, 50-foot canvas. She was very angry when the completed mural was hung so high that people could hardly see the result of her labors. And to make matters worse, the organizers in Chicago lost the painting after the World's Fair closed.

"I am determined that women should be someone and not something." (Mary Cassatt)

Despite her success in France, Cassatt received very little recognition in her homeland. When she returned to her native America in 1898—her first visit in more than 20 years—the local press only reported: "Mary Cassatt … returned from Europe yesterday. She has been studying painting in France and owns the smallest pekinese dog in the world."

Cassatt was very upset by this lack of appreciation of her paintings in America, particularly as the work of the other Impressionists was selling well there. She did start to build up a reputation for herself a few years later, following an exhibit of her work at Durand-Ruel's New York gallery in 1903. By this time, however, the artist was back in Europe.

In later years, Cassatt divided most of her time between her Paris apartment and her summer home, the Château de Beaufresne, a 17th-century manor house 50 miles from Paris. This routine was only broken during World War I, between 1914 and 1918, when the threat of German invasion made her evacuate to Grasse, in the south of France. She received many honors later in life, the most important being the French Legion of Honor in 1904.

THE FINAL YEARS

Cassatt's final years were troubled. The death of her brother, Gardner, in 1911, prompted a nervous collapse. Her eyesight began to fail, gradually making it impossible for her to paint. In 1914, she was awarded a Gold Medal of Honor from the Pennsylvania Academy of Fine Arts, where she had studied as a young woman. She died alone at her château in June 1926. By the time she died, she was completely blind.

MAJOR WORKS

1868	THE MANDOLIN PLAYER
1878	LITTLE GIRL IN A BLUE ARMCHAIR
1879	AT THE OPERA
1893-94	THE BOATING PARTY
1894	SUMMERTIME
1905	MOTHER AND CHILD

PAUL GAUGUIN

One of the most revolutionary painters of the 19th century, Gauguin was as unconventional in his art as he was in his lifestyle. His bold, uncompromising work inspired generations of future artists.

Paul Gauguin was born in Paris on June 7, 1848. Later that year, his parents decided to travel to Peru, where Paul's Peruvian-born mother, Aline, had relatives. In 1849, they set sail from France. Paul's father, Clovis, died of a heart attack on the journey. Aline, with Paul and his sister, Marie, spent the next six years living in Peru. Then, Paul's grandfather died back in France, and the family returned to take up their inheritance in the old man's hometown of Orléans, in central France.

A TASTE FOR ADVENTURE

Paul hated Orléans. He found it dull and depressing compared with his colorful, exotic life in Peru. By the time he was 17, the boy was restless. He longed for adventure. In 1865, he went to sea and worked for three years on a merchant vessel before joining the navy in 1868.

When he was 23, Gauguin left the navy. He found a job as an assistant to a leading Paris stockbroker. A wealthy future lay ahead. In 1873, Gauguin married a Danish woman, Mette Sophie Gad. By 1883, Gauguin had money, a business reputation, a good home, and five children.

THE IMPRESSIONISTS

During this period, Gauguin began to paint as a hobby. Through business colleagues, Gauguin had met several Impressionist painters, and had started to buy their work. In 1874, he studied with a leading Impressionist, Camille Pissarro (*see page 8*), and his work began to move toward the Impressionist style. From 1879 onward, he exhibited at all the Impressionist group shows.

By this time, Gauguin was thinking about becoming a full-time painter. His paintings attracted praise, and sold well, too. Then, in 1883, France's stock market crashed. Suddenly, Gauguin's job no longer looked secure. Confident

Self-portrait, 1890, by Paul Gauguin
The 42-year-old artist shows himself in a thoughtful pose. The painting shows his use of vibrant colors and bold line.

that he could support his family by painting, he resigned.

The country's financial collapse had affected the art market, too, however. In a year, Gauguin had sold only one or two paintings. His savings were gone, and his family was nearly destitute. His wife, Mette, now took control of the Gauguins' future. She insisted that they move to her native Denmark.

RETURNING TO PARIS

But their move was a failure. Although Gauguin found a job as a salesman, he disliked the work and sold little. Once again, he turned toward painting. In 1885, he left once more for Paris, leaving Mette with four of his children in Denmark. He took his six-year-old son, Clovis, with him.

By the winter of 1885, Gauguin was penniless. He and his son lived in one small room. Cold and underfed, the boy became ill. To feed him, Gauguin found work putting up advertisements for a railroad company. Clovis recovered and Gauguin sent him back to Mette in Denmark. From now on, he would see his family very rarely. He had basically abandoned them to their own fate.

A LONG STRUGGLE

In June 1886, Gauguin moved once more, to Pont-Aven in Brittany, in the northwest of France. There, he found a cheap place to stay, a group of appreciative fellow-artists, and the seclusion that he needed to work. But, although his confidence was growing, there was little opportunity for financial success in Pont-Aven.

GAUGUIN'S COLOR

Gauguin developed a powerful style using non-realistic color and simple shapes to express feelings.

The Impressionists had painted the natural world with vividness and directness. But Gauguin wanted to express intense emotions rather than depict the world around him in a realistic or straightforward way. So he developed a new style using bold shapes and vivid colors.

Unlike the Impressionists, who built up their colors with small, energetic dashes of paint, Gauguin used large areas of flat, unbroken color. When he was painting in Brittany, in the northwest of France, he often separated these areas with thick dark lines. But in many of his Tahitian paintings he simply

At the end of 1886, he returned to Paris, where he almost starved during the winter. The following year, he decided to make a complete break. "Paris," he wrote, "is a desert for a poor man. I must get my energy back, and I'm going to Panama to live like a native."

Somehow, he managed to find the fare. Once in Panama, in South Central America, he worked as a laborer on a

butted one area of intense color up against another (*above*).

Gauguin often used color in an unnaturalistic way to set the emotional tone of a picture. He refused to be limited by any conventions in his art. In his painting, *The Yellow Christ*, painted in 1889, for example, the color is totally unreal. The yellow body of Christ, outlined in thick black lines, and the red trees stress the otherworldliness of the crucifixion scene.

French project to build the Panama Canal. But, after a few weeks, he caught yellow fever and moved on to Martinique, in the French West Indies. Four months later, ill-health and poverty forced him back to France, and he returned to Brittany.

This was a vital period for Gauguin. For the first time, he broke away from the influence of Impressionism. The

Impressionists wanted to show the way things looked. Gauguin, however, did not believe that a painting had to show the real world. He wanted his art to express strong emotions, and was more interested in ideas than what things looked like. To achieve such intense feeling, he had to develop a new style of painting.

NEW INSPIRATION

Gauguin looked for inspiration from ancient Egyptian and medieval sculpture, and from prehistoric Central and South American art. Unlike the Impressionists, who built up colors with small, energetic dashes of paint, he used

> "I have decided on Tahiti ... and I hope to cultivate my art there in the wild and primitive state."
> (Paul Gauguin, 1890s)

large areas of bold, unbroken color, often separated by dark lines. At the age of 40, Gauguin was at last producing great and original work.

TO ARLES

In October 1888, he accepted an invitation to spend the winter in Arles, in southern France, with the Dutch painter, Vincent van Gogh (*see page 62*), whom he had met two years earlier in

Two Tahitian Women on a Beach, 1891, by Paul Gauguin
Two women laze silently on a sandy beach, in a mood of timelessness. To express an intensity of feeling, Gauguin uses flat areas of bold, vital color.

Paris. But Gauguin had been in Arles for only around two months when during an argument, the mentally unbalanced van Gogh threatened him with a razor. Gauguin returned immediately to Paris.

SYMBOLISM

Over the next few years, Gauguin spent his time in Paris and Brittany. His reputation among other artists had never been higher. By 1889, he was the central figure in a new movement called Symbolism, which focused on the expression of ideas, moods, and emotions.

But Gauguin was still desperately poor. He yearned to leave Europe and return to the tropics. On April 1, 1891,

he sailed to Tahiti, a French colony in the South Seas. To pay for the trip, he sold all his paintings at very low prices.

At first, the island was not the exotic paradise Gauguin had expected. The Tahitian capital, Papeete, was just like a small French coastal town, only more boring. "It was Europe all over again," he wrote. Thirty miles farther inland, however, he found the peace he wanted. There, he lived among native islanders, sharing a hut with a young Tahitian girl.

SOUTH SEA INSPIRATION

The bright lights and strong colors of Tahiti, together with the exotic beauty of the islanders, made a huge impact on

Gauguin. He painted them again and again during this period. Rejecting the ideas that a painting had to represent something we can see in the real world, he used strong colors to express his feelings about the tropical island. Gauguin chose colors for their decorative as well as expressive effect—they appeal to the eye as well as helping to create a mood, atmosphere, or feeling.

RETURNING HOME

Although his art was progressing, money was still a problem. Despite his dreams, Gauguin could not live for free. He could not fish or farm, and so he had to buy expensive, imported European food. A period of illness reduced his savings yet further. In 1893, he had to return to France.

It was a humiliating return for Gauguin, but the pictures he brought back persuaded a leading Paris dealer to give him an exhibit. The paintings did not sell well, but Gauguin's new work excited other artists. He also received a financial windfall: An uncle had died and left the painter enough money to set up a studio in Paris. Gauguin was determined to return to Tahiti, however, and in July 1895 he left France for the last time.

A DIFFICULT TIME

Back in Tahiti, Gauguin was producing some of his greatest art, again painting the Tahitians that he lived with. But his life was often miserable. Most of the time he was short of money, and his health steadily worsened. In March 1897, he learned that his 20-year-old daughter had died in Denmark. Although he had neglected his family for years, he was devastated by the news. His despair drove him to a failed suicide attempt later that year.

A LASTING INFLUENCE

In 1901, Gauguin left Tahiti and traveled 800 miles to the Marquesas Islands, where he settled in the village of Atuona. There, he built his last home, which he called "The House of Pleasure." At last Gauguin was working happily as well as very hard. His creative output had had a terrible effect on his health, though. On May 8, 1903, Gauguin died, aged 54.

By the time of his death, the art world back in France had virtually forgotten Gauguin. Over the following decade, however, a series of exhibits in Paris and London firmly established his lasting reputation as one of the most important influences on early 20th-century art.

MAJOR WORKS

1888	VISION AFTER THE SERMON
1889	THE YELLOW CHRIST
1891	TWO TAHITIAN WOMEN ON A BEACH
1894	THE DAY OF THE GOD
1897	WHERE DO WE COME FROM? WHAT ARE WE? WHERE ARE WE GOING TO?
1898	THE WHITE HORSE

VINCENT VAN GOGH

Although van Gogh only painted for the last decade of his life, in those few, tormented years he worked day and night to produce more than 800 pictures. Using blazes of thick, bold colors, he expressed his love of nature.

Vincent Willem van Gogh was born on March 30, 1853, in Groot Zundert, a small Dutch village near the border with Belgium. He was a moody and difficult child who liked to be alone. He rarely played with his younger brother, Theo, or his three little sisters. Instead, he spent his time drawing.

When Vincent left school in 1869, he went to work for one of his uncles, an art dealer in The Hague, a major Dutch city. After working there for four years, Vincent was transferred to the London branch of the business. In London, he fell in love with his landlady's daughter. The affair was a disaster. Vincent was very upset, and his work suffered. In the end, he was fired and returned home.

In 1876, he returned to England to work in a school. He had the job of collecting fees in some of London's poorest areas. The poverty he saw distressed him so much that he failed to collect a single penny. He resigned.

This experience awakened a religious fervor in him and he became an assistant to a Methodist minister. He enjoyed the work, and returned to Holland to train for the ministry in 1877. Although he gave up after a year, his passionate desire to spread the gospel remained. A year later, he moved to the Borinage, a coal-mining district in Belgium, to work as a preacher.

The hardship he found there was even worse than in London. Van Gogh threw himself into his work with such enthusiasm that he gave away his clothes and food to the poor. His superiors were appalled by his fanatic behavior. Again, he was fired.

ARTISTIC VOCATION

After two more years in the Borinage, van Gogh returned home to his parents in 1880. He now had a new mission: to become an artist. He threw himself into the task with the same passion he

Self-portrait, 1889, by Vincent van Gogh
Van Gogh shows himself with a bandage on his ear, which he cut off after an argument with his friend, the artist Paul Gauguin.

had brought to evangelism. But his temperament was becoming increasingly unstable. After a quarrel with his father on Christmas Day in 1881, Vincent left home and again moved to The Hague.

With no money to live on, Vincent had to ask his brother for help. Theo sent him something each month from his own small salary, but it was not enough. In 1884, once again van Gogh was forced to return home to his parents. There, he painted *The Potato Eaters*, a dark and gloomy painting of peasants at their meager evening meal.

A MOVE TO PARIS

In 1886, his father died and van Gogh left Holland, never to return. After a brief stay in Belgium, he moved into Theo's apartment in Montmartre, the artists' quarter of Paris. Van Gogh discovered the work of the Impressionists. Their bright colors appealed to him. He now abandoned the somber browns and blacks he had used in Holland.

Through Theo, who was now working as an art dealer, van Gogh met Camille Pissarro and Paul Gauguin (*see pages 8 and 56*). He also studied for a few months with Henri de Toulouse-Lautrec (*see page 74*).

During this period, van Gogh's art developed rapidly. But he was very unhappy. Unlike the Parisians, whom he found cold and reserved, he had a passionate, changeable temper. After two years in Paris, he declared: "I will take myself off somewhere down south."

In 1888, he moved to Arles, a small city near Marseilles in the south of

THE POWER OF COLOR

Van Gogh used thick layers of paint to exaggerate his blazes of vibrant color and express his strong feelings.

Early in his career, van Gogh used the Impressionist technique of applying paint in small dashes. But later, he painted in waves and swirls (*above right*). He piled the paint on so thickly that the marks stand above the canvas. He often squeezed it straight from the tube onto the picture, then modeled it a little with his brush. This thickly applied paint—known as *impasto*—remained a hallmark of van Gogh's work until his death.

Another characteristic of his was the use of bold, expressive colors. For van Gogh, colors did not merely describe objects, but gave them meaning and feeling.

France. He rented a house known as the Yellow House, so-called because its outside walls were painted yellow. Van Gogh was ecstatically happy there, the brilliant Mediterranean sunlight filling him with inspiration. "Ideas," he wrote to Theo, "are coming to me in swarms."

For over a year, van Gogh worked and worked, producing hundreds of landscapes, still lifes, and portraits.

His letters to Theo reveal the artist's favorite colors: He always began by asking Theo to send large tubes of yellow and white paint.

No color meant more to van Gogh than yellow. He believed that it represented the glory of the sun and golden wheat—that it was the color of creation. He painted his pictures of sun-flowers almost entirely in yellow. All the other colors he used—especially purple and blue—served only to increase the power of his favorite color.

Sometimes he painted for up to 16 hours a day. He had always worked in frenzied bursts of activity, but now he hardly stopped to eat or drink.

MENTAL BREAKDOWN

Van Gogh wanted to set up an artists' colony at Arles. The first person he asked to join was his old friend Paul Gauguin, who arrived in October 1888.

But the two men were soon quarreling. At Christmas, passions reached a head and van Gogh threatened Gauguin with a razor. Gauguin took shelter in a hotel. The fight marked the beginning of a long period of mental instability for van Gogh. That night, he cut off part of his right ear. Suffering from loss of

> "I am not conscious of myself any more, and the pictures come to me as if in a dream." (Vincent van Gogh)

blood and hallucinations, he was taken to a hospital. He was released after two weeks, but overwork brought on a relapse. When he finally returned to his Yellow House in Arles, he found he was unwelcome: 80 locals had signed a petition demanding that the "madman" be put away in an asylum.

SHATTERED HOPES

Within just a year of his arrival in Arles, all of his hopes and optimism had been shattered. Gauguin had fled back to Paris, and van Gogh's plans for an artists' colony were in tatters. He dreaded the return of his mental illness so much that he left Arles and committed himself to an asylum.

He was probably suffering from epilepsy or schizophrenia, but cold baths were the only treatment he received. Despite bouts of convulsions and

Starry Night, 1889, by Vincent van Gogh
Van Gogh painted several "starry night" pictures. In this vibrant version, the artist uses dramatic swirling circles of thick yellow and white paint against a brilliant blue sky in order to depict light from the larger-than-life stars and crescent moon. The huge cypress tree seems to writhe with energy.

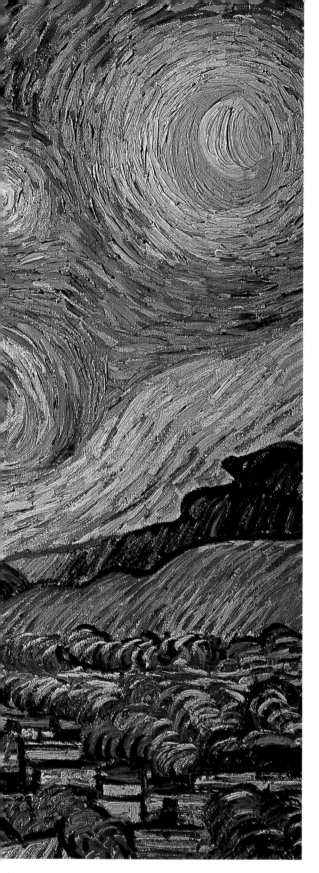

hallucinations, he produced some 200 canvases during his year in the asylum.

In 1890, Theo wrote to Vincent to tell him that one of his paintings had been sold in an auction. It was the only work he sold during his lifetime. Shortly after, van Gogh decided to leave the south and moved to Auvers, a village north-west of Paris. He was placed in the care of Dr. Gachet, who had experience in treating mental disorders.

At first, van Gogh seemed in good spirits. He was painting steadily and he took a room at the local café. But in July, a conversation with Theo about money worried him. He felt he was a financial drain on his brother.

On July 27, 1890, van Gogh walked out into the Auvers countryside and shot himself in the chest. He then walked home and went to bed, where he lay awake all night, smoking his pipe. The following day, Vincent van Gogh died in his devoted brother's arms. He was 37.

MAJOR WORKS

1885	THE POTATO EATERS
1888	SUNFLOWERS; CAFÉ TERRACE AT NIGHT; THE SOWER; THE NIGHT CAFÉ
1889	STARRY NIGHT; THE ARTIST'S BEDROOM AT ARLES; SELF-PORTRAIT WITH BANDAGED EAR; WHEATFIELD WITH CYPRESSES
1890	PORTRAIT OF DR. GACHET

GEORGES SEURAT

Best known for his novel technique of painting in tiny dots of color, Georges Seurat devoted his short life entirely to art. He was intensely secretive, jealously guarding his latest ideas from even his closest friends.

Georges Seurat was born in Paris on December 2, 1859. His mother was quiet and affectionate, but his father, a legal official, was a solitary man with a surly character.

As a young man, Seurat was tall and handsome, with "velvety eyes" and a quiet, gentle voice. Like his father, he liked to keep to himself, and he was very secretive. He was serious and intense by nature, often preferring to buy books rather than food or drink.

In 1878, Seurat entered the School of Fine Arts, the official Paris art school. He was a model student of the academic style and his early drawings showed the influence of traditional artists such as Jean-August-Dominique Ingres. In 1879, a year of compulsory military service interrupted his artistic studies. He was stationed in Brest, a military port in northwest France. Whenever he was off duty, he would go down to the harbor to sketch the ships.

After his year in the army, Seurat returned to Paris to resume his training.

He shared a cramped studio with two friends, before moving to his own studio close to his parents' home. His family was well-off and provided him with financial support. This meant that, unlike his fellow artists, Seurat could concentrate on developing his art in the way he wanted, without the worry of having to sell pictures to survive. For the next two years, he devoted himself to drawing in black and white.

SEURAT'S BATHERS

Seurat spent 1883 working on his first major work, *Bathers at Asnières*. The huge painting showed working people relaxing at the weekend near Asnières, an industrial town outside Paris. In the painting, the air is heavy with mid-summer heat, and the people have come to the banks of the Seine River to cool off. The simple, static poses of the

Georges Seurat, 1890s
This photograph shows the reserved and serious young artist in the early 1890s, shortly before his death at the age of 31.

figures give the painting an air of calm and silence. Only one boy in the water, frozen in the act of cupping his hands to his mouth, seems to make a sound. Seurat painted the work with short strokes of color, which he placed next to each other to build up shapes.

LASTING DETERMINATION

Delighted with his *Bathers*, Seurat sent the painting to the 1884 Salon, the official state exhibit, only to see the jury reject it. This disappointment did not discourage Seurat, however. He was very determined, and had a single-minded approach to his work. He was convinced of the importance of his paintings. In May 1884, he sent the canvas to an independent exhibit taking place in a temporary hut near the Tuileries Palace in central Paris.

The show ended in a financial mess, but it resulted in the birth of the Society of Independent Artists. The group was committed to holding an exhibit each year that, unlike the Salon, would have no jury. Seurat attended its meetings regularly, always sitting in the same seat, quietly smoking his pipe.

At one meeting, Seurat met Paul Signac. Four years younger than Seurat, Signac was a self-taught painter who followed the style of the Impressionists. Outgoing and enthusiastic, he provided Seurat with several contacts and supported the older painter as he tried to make his mark on the Paris art scene.

In the summer of 1884, Seurat embarked on another major canvas, *Sunday on the Island of La Grande Jatte*. Again depicting Asnières, this

DABS OF COLOR

With the aid of scientific research papers on color, Seurat developed a highly original method of painting.

In *Sunday on the Island of La Grande Jatte*, Seurat used his novel technique of painting in regular dabs of brilliant paint, which he developed after reading scientific theories of color. The artist called this method Divisionism, but it is also known as Pointillism.

Instead of mixing his colors on the palette, Seurat placed thousands of tiny, separate dots of unmixed color side by side on the canvas (*above right*). In theory, the colors would then mix in the eye of the viewer, without losing their brilliance.

Using this method, Seurat tried to capture subtle effects of

time he focused on *La Grande Jatte*, a little island in the Seine. Every morning for months, Seurat would travel to his chosen spot by the river and sketch with complete concentration. In the afternoon, he would shut himself away in his studio to continue work on the vast, 10-foot canvas. Perched on a ladder and surrounded by books, he painted in complete silence, with his

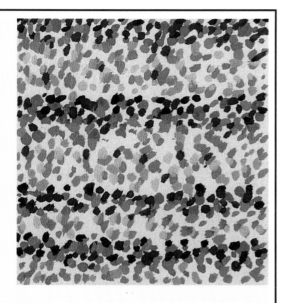

light in his paintings. He hoped not only to achieve greater accuracy of detail, but also to represent the way that colors vibrate in strong sunlight.

Seurat's method of painting was slow and extremely meticulous, almost scientific. He liked to leave nothing to chance, and never started a picture unless he knew exactly how it would finish. As one friend remarked, "The sensation of being carried away meant nothing to him."

eyes half closed. He often worked late into the night, unconcerned by the poor light in his studio. If he wanted a breath of fresh air, he would go for long walks around Paris. After two years of painstaking work, Seurat finally completed the painting.

It showed fashionable Parisians relaxing on the island on a sunny Sunday afternoon. Seurat delighted in showing the finest details of their clothes, their hats and canes, dainty fans, and genteel reading-material.

PAINTING WITH DOTS

La Grande Jatte was the first major work in which Seurat used his new, revolutionary technique of painting. Known as Pointillism, it involved placing thousands of tiny, multicolored dots of paint on the canvas to suggest the vibrancy of strong sunlight. When Seurat exhibited the painting with the Impressionist group in May 1886, it caused a sensation. Although some people criticized the work, others believed that Seurat was providing the most significant way forward from Impressionism. His admirers called him the "Messiah of a new art."

Suddenly, Seurat found that he was the most controversial artist in Paris. He moved to a new studio near Signac's on Boulevard de Clichy in Montmartre, the artistic quarter of Paris. The studio was a popular meeting place for independent artists, both young and old, including Edgar Degas, Paul Gauguin, Vincent van Gogh, and Henri de Toulouse-Lautrec (*see pages 20, 56, 62, and 74*).

A SIMPLE ATTITUDE

Seurat's financial security meant that he was not used to dealing with clients, and his demands for payment remained relatively modest, despite his new fame. His attitude to his work was similarly down-to-earth. When critics described his work as poetic, he said: "No, I apply my method and that is all."

Yet he did not want to lose credit for his new pointillist technique and he guarded its secrets obsessively.

WORKING HABITS

Seurat's life had begun to assume a regular pattern. During the winter months, he locked himself away in his studio, working on a large picture to exhibit in the spring. He spent the summer months on the Normandy coast "to freshen his eyes," working on smaller, less complex seascapes.

Whether in Paris or on the coast, the artist was never a great socializer. When friends came to visit, they found him reserved and uncommunicative. He only became excited when they talked about his ideas and theories.

From 1887 onward, Seurat turned his restless attention to the problem of drawing lines. He learned that these could express different emotions depending on the direction they pointed: upward-slanting lines express happiness, horizontal lines suggest calm, and downward-sloping lines

MAJOR WORKS	
1883-84	BATHERS AT ASNIÈRES
1885	BOATS AT GRANDCHAMP
1884-86	SUNDAY AFTERNOON ON THE ISLAND OF LA GRANDE JATTE
1890	THE CHANNEL AT GRAVELINES, EVENING
1890-91	THE CIRCUS

create a sad effect. He applied these theories in some of his later works, especially those depicting the high-spirited world of the circus.

A SECRET FAMILY

Late in 1889, Seurat moved away from the bustling Boulevard de Clichy to a studio in a quieter street nearby. Unknown to his family and friends, from whom he had now virtually cut

Bathers at Asnières, 1883-1884, by Georges Seurat
Seurat shows workers relaxing by the Seine River after a hard day in the factories, which are in the distance. He later retouched the painting in his famous pointillist style.

himself off, he lived there with a young model, Madeleine Knobloch. In February 1890, Madeleine gave birth in the studio to a son. Seurat legally acknowledged the child, and gave him his own Christian names in reverse, Pierre-Georges. But he kept his young family a secret from his mother.

In March 1891, Seurat died unexpectedly at the age of 31. It seems that he had contracted a form of meningitis. But his loyal fellow-artist Paul Signac sadly concluded, "Our poor friend has killed himself by overwork." Seurat was buried in the Père-Lachaise cemetery in Paris.

HENRI DE TOULOUSE-LAUTREC

Rejecting his wealthy upbringing, Toulouse-Lautrec's art captured the lively bars and nightclubs of Paris where he felt most at home. With his deft skill and sharp eye, he created works full of color, humor, and energy.

Henri de Toulouse-Lautrec was born on November 24, 1864, in Albi, southwest France. His parents came from one of the oldest aristocratic families in the country, and were enormously wealthy. Yet, despite his privileged childhood, life was not easy for the boy.

When he was a teenager, he broke both his legs. Rather than healing properly, the bones stopped growing. They would remain fragile for the rest of his life. As his upper body developed normally, Henri looked more and more stunted and misshapen. But instead of feeling sorry for himself, he threw himself into his great love—drawing. Encouraged by both his father and his uncle, who were keen amateur artists, the boy soon had his own art tutor.

A DISTINCTIVE FIGURE

In 1882, Lautrec moved to the capital city, Paris, with his mother. There, he joined an artist's workshop and studied hard. During the next three years, the young painter became well known in the city's art world, as much for his personality and appearance as for his great talent. People always recognized Lautrec. He was only 5-feet tall, always carried a walking stick, wore a bowler hat, and had little glasses on the end of his nose.

At first, he lived with friends of his parents. But he was desperate to live a bohemian, or unconventional, life in Montmartre. This was the quarter where most artists lived and worked, and it was the city's entertainment and social center. In 1886, Lautrec's parents gave him enough money to set up a studio there. He shared an apartment near the studio with a friend.

Lautrec threw himself into Parisian nightlife with great energy and enthusiasm. Every night, he was up until dawn drinking, talking, and watching

Toulouse-Lautrec at his desk, 1898, by Édouard Vuillard
This affectionate portrait of the artist by his friend shows his small stature.

74

people having fun. He loved the bars and cafés, the dance halls and cabarets, and the circuses and theaters. These places became Lautrec's main source of inspiration. He was thrilled and excited by the color, energy, and movement he saw around him.

Lautrec's particular skill was in drawing—he could capture the movement and energy of a busy scene, or a character, with just a simple silhouette, an outline, and a few patches of color. He preferred to paint scenes from real life rather than formal, posed subjects. He had a sharp sense of humor, and captured personalities in a simple and bold way, almost like in a cartoon.

In 1888, Lautrec began to enjoy some success. He exhibited his paintings with a group of modern artists called *Les Vingt*—The Twenty—and the following year he took part in an exhibit for the Society of Independent Artists, which was the most important show for ambitious young artists.

THE LITHOGRAPHS

Besides painting, Lautrec also began to make lithographs. Lithography is a fairly simple printing technique in which the artist makes a drawing with a greasy pencil or crayon on a slab of limestone. Water is then applied to the stone. It sinks into the areas which are free from grease. Next, ink is rolled over the slab. The ink attaches to the drawing but not the wet areas. A piece of paper is then placed on top of the stone and the whole thing is put through a printing press. The final image is the reverse of the original.

THE MOULIN ROUGE

The lively evenings at the Paris nightclub, the Moulin Rouge, provided Lautrec with exciting subject matter.

Named for its "red mill" which was lit up at night (*right*), the Moulin Rouge opened in Montmartre, Paris, in 1889. Its vast dancefloor, glittering lights, and exotic entertainment attracted Parisians of all classes.

There was plenty to see and do at the Moulin Rouge. A circus-like din of music set the tone for the evening, as patrons and performers took the floor together, dancing energetically. A variety of entertainers appeared each night, including clowns, singers, exotic dancers, acrobats, and cancan troupes. At the back of the club, a huge cardboard elephant dominated a

Like several of his fellow artists, including the Dutch painter, Vincent van Gogh (*see page 62*), Lautrec was influenced by the bold and colorful designs of Japanese prints, which were very popular in Paris at the time. Following their example, Lautrec tended to use just a few colors and simple outlines in his lithographs, making them very striking images.

garden, where patrons could take donkey rides. The elephant could hold an entire orchestra.

An English reporter described the typical raucous scene at the club: "In this place no passions need be curbed. There is shouting and horseplay; women are carried around the hall on the shoulders of men; there is a fierce increasing cry for drink."

Toulouse-Lautrec was a regular patron of the club from its opening night, and found the intense, vulgar scene, and the lively female dancers, ideal material for his art.

This approach is evident in Lautrec's most influential works, his poster designs. These posters usually advertised a person, such as an actor or a singer, or a place of entertainment. Lautrec would sit in the dark, smoky atmosphere of a club or bar, sketching rapidly in order to capture the movement and color of the scene before him. To help him work more quickly, he used thinner oil paint; this allowed him to "draw" with his brushes.

Lautrec's first great poster, *La Goulue*, was for the Moulin Rouge, a popular nightclub that opened in 1889. The poster showed one of the club's star cancan dancers called Louise Weber, who was also known as "La Goulue," or "the greedy one," and her partner Valentin Désossé. Lautrec portrayed the dancer kicking her legs high into the air during one of her extraordinary, athletic performances.

> ## "I have tried to draw something real, not something ideal." (Toulouse-Lautrec in a letter to his mother)

Valentin—whose surname means "boneless"—appears as a sinister, top-hatted silhouette in front of her.

La Goulue immediately made Lautrec famous as the leading poster artist in Paris. No one had ever seen anything like his advertisements before. They were new and exciting. They often had odd viewpoints, which made them look like snapshots taken in an instant, even though they were in fact the result of many carefully prepared sketches. Parisians noticed these striking images at once as they walked through the city's crowded streets.

La Goulue, 1891, by Henri de Toulouse-Lautrec
Lautrec's poster advertising the Moulin Rouge shows his favorite cancan dancer, the 20-year-old "La Goulue," with her distinctive knot of hair on her head. The customers of the club appear as a row of silhouetted hats in the background.

Lautrec's social life was exhausting. Often, he would arrive at the workshop in Montmartre still wearing his evening clothes from the night before. But even when he had not slept, he would work through the entire day without a break, carefully printing his lithographs.

With his success, Lautrec began to make new acquaintances in the art world. His friends now included the

> "I am hampered by a host of sentimental ties that I must forget if I want to achieve anything."
> (Toulouse-Lautrec)

artists Pierre Bonnard and Édouard Vuillard. Both painters provided illustrations for *La Revue Blanche—The White Review*—a modern art magazine. Lautrec fell in love with Misia Natanson, the wife of the man who owned the magazine. She had the kind of flamboyant personality that he adored.

By the 1890s, Lautrec's lifestyle was beginning to harm his health. He was drinking too much and driving himself too hard. In 1893, he moved back into his mother's apartment. His drunken behavior caused tension in the family, who reduced his allowance, so that he had to work for a living.

His friends tried to help him. One old schoolfriend, Maurice Joyant, took him

MAJOR WORKS

1888	AT THE CIRCUS FERNANDO
1890	THE DANCE AT THE MOULIN ROUGE
1891	LA GOULUE
1892	ARISTIDE BRUANT AT THE AMBASSADEURS; AT THE MOULIN ROUGE
1894	THE SALON AT THE RUE DES MOULINS

sailing on weekends, and in 1898 arranged a one-man exhibit for Lautrec at a gallery in London. But he had lost interest in his art and the show was a dismal failure. And his health was getting steadily worse. The following year, he had a severe attack of *delirium tremens*—alcoholic shaking and hallucinations. His mother had him admitted to a clinic in Neuilly, just outside Paris.

AN EARLY DEATH

Shocked to find himself in a hospital, Lautrec took up drawing again, mainly doing colorful circus scenes from memory. When he left the clinic, he went to stay with a cousin, Paul Viaud, who looked after him, taking him to the opera and to the coast.

But Lautrec was too ill to enjoy these treats. He was only 36, but looked like an old man. In the summer of 1901, while on vacation near Bordeaux, the artist collapsed. His mother took him to her house at Malromé, where he died on September 9, 1901.

ÉMILE ZOLA

One of the greatest French novelists of his time, Zola pioneered a new style called Naturalism, which sought to portray people in a very realistic way. His work was influential, forming the basis of the modern novel.

Émile Zola was born in Paris on April 2, 1840. He was the only child of Francesco, an Italian engineer, and Émilie. In 1843, the family moved to Aix-en-Provence in the south of France, where Francesco had won a contract to improve the town's water supply. Zola's father died just four years later, however, leaving Émilie to bring up her son in near-poverty. Somehow, she found the money to send him to the local school.

BEGINNING TO WRITE

In 1858, Zola moved to Paris to complete his education. A long illness hindered his progress, however, and he failed to gain his diploma. As a result, he was forced to take on a succession of poorly paid jobs in order to make a living. The next few years were miserable, but they did provide Zola with much of the material that would later fill his novels. He had already begun to write, mostly poems rather than stories.

Zola entered the world of books in 1862, when he became a clerk at Hachette's, a large publishing firm in Paris. He remained there for four years. The job was dull, but it enabled Zola to support himself while he developed his writing. He completed his first novel, *Claude's Confession*, in 1865. A year later, he left Hachette to devote himself fully to literature.

At first, he worked as a journalist, making his mark with a series of controversial articles supporting the painter Édouard Manet (*see page 14*), who was unpopular at the time. Zola earned extra money by churning out melodramatic tales which were serialized in the newspapers.

This was a good way for a writer to build up a reputation. Improvements in education had brought about a huge increase in literacy in the mid-19th

Portrait of Émile Zola, 1868,
by Édouard Manet
Manet shows the writer at his desk. To the right is the article Zola wrote on the artist.

century. These new readers created a demand for popular fiction. Many of the recently educated people came from the poorer sections of society, and wanted a different kind of book. They were not interested in the historical romances or the dramas that were written for the leisured classes. They wanted to read about people who were like themselves: people who worked in factories, lived in cheap housing, and were always short of money.

A MODERN APPROACH

Zola offered them precisely what they wanted. His first novel of real quality, *Thérèse Raquin*, concerned an ordinary shopkeeper caught up in a horrific tale of adultery, murder, and revenge. These events were dramatic, yet the Parisian setting and the everyday lives of the characters seemed familiar to his readers, helping them to understand and relate to the novel.

The book sold well, but old-fashioned critics were outraged, accusing Zola of catering to the lowest possible tastes. The novelist defended himself in the preface to the second edition of the novel. His explanation of his motives effectively outlined the principles of the Naturalist movement.

His approach, he argued, had been a scientific one. He had wanted to show how his "human animals," as he called them, were driven to their actions by their very nature. He had tried to analyze them with the same detachment as a surgeon dissecting a corpse.

Zola developed these ideas over the next few years, hoping to apply them on

ZOLA AND CÉZANNE

Zola was friends with the great artist, Paul Cézanne. But the friendship was competitive and turbulent.

Zola had strong connections with the art world. In his youth, he championed the paintings of Manet, and mixed with the artists in the Impressionist circle. His closest link, however, was with his boyhood friend, the artist Paul Cézanne (*see page 32*). Cézanne painted a friend, Paul Alexis, reading to Zola, in about 1869 (*above right*).

They had both attended the same school at Aix, where it was Émile rather than Paul who won a drawing prize. Later, their friendship continued in Paris, as they struggled to establish themselves in their chosen fields, and they encouraged each other.

a much grander scale. He conceived the idea of writing a huge cycle of novels—the Rougon-Macquart series—in which he would tell the story of his times through the fortunes of a single family.

The first of these books, *The Fortune of the Rougons*, was being serialized just as the Franco-Prussian War broke out in 1870. Publication was halted, as Zola fled south to Marseilles with his

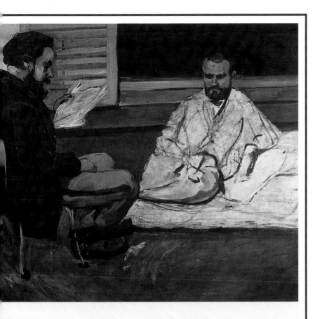

In spite of their shared hardships, however, the two men were very different. Zola was ambitious, and slightly jealous of Cézanne's wealthier background, while the latter could be moody and withdrawn.

Their friendship ended in 1886, when Zola wrote a novel called *L'Oeuvre—The Masterpiece*—about a failed artist who is driven to suicide. Cézanne felt that the book was about him and, deeply hurt, he refused to see the writer ever again.

of the characters but, in reality, each story was separate. The true linking factor was Zola's "scientific" approach. He continued to argue that his characters had no control over their fate, which was shaped by a combination of hereditary and social conditions.

Modern critics, however, reject the author's claims to scientific detachment. They point out that Zola was actually a very emotional writer, and that his personality is stamped firmly on all his creations. They praise him for the way in which he brought to life such a broad cross section of French society.

In most cases, the emphasis was on the darker side of life. In *The Drink*

> "I have chosen people dominated by their nerves and blood ... drawn to each action ... by their nature."
> (Émile Zola)

mother and his new bride, Alexandrine. For a brief spell, he worked as a secretary to a government official in Bordeaux, before returning to Paris in 1871, anxious to revive the project.

The 20 books of the series, published over a 22-year period, from 1871 to 1893, form the backbone of Zola's literary career. In theory, the books were linked by the family connections

Shop, Zola portrayed a laundress who is dragged down into poverty by her drunken husband; *Germinal* is a compelling study of the passions aroused by a miners' strike; while *The Human Animal* is a murder story set against the backdrop of the newly built railroads, which implies that mankind's actions would always be guided by its most basic instincts, no matter how advanced it might appear to be.

Nana, 1877, by Édouard Manet
Manet's painting depicts Nana, the heroine of Zola's 1880 novel of the same name. The
book charts the moral decay of a beautiful but untalented actress. Nana builds herself
up from nothing to become part of wealthy society, which then destroys her. To the right
of the picture is one of Nana's many male admirers, dressed in smart evening clothes.

Throughout his career Zola's novels sold very well, even though they continued to attract violent criticism. Right-wing reviewers attacked him for reveling in sex, violence, and crime. From other quarters, he was blamed for showing the working classes in an unfavorable light.

Zola completed the last of the series of Rougon-Macquart books, *Doctor Pascal*, in 1893. In his final years, he devised two smaller cycles of novels.

"I applied to two living bodies the analytical method that surgeons apply to corpses."
(Émile Zola)

The first of these dealt with three cities, while the novelist described the second group as his "Four Gospels." He only completed three of the "gospels," however, dealing with the themes of Fertility, Labor, and Truth. He would die before tackling the fourth, Justice.

THE DREYFUS AFFAIR

These late works were overshadowed by Zola's involvement in a notorious political scandal, the so-called Dreyfus Affair. In 1894, Alfred Dreyfus, a Jewish officer in the French army, was found guilty of treason and sentenced to life imprisonment. It later became clear that another soldier had committed the crime. But the military authorities tried to suppress the evidence, seemingly for anti-Semitic reasons.

The case provoked a public outcry, and Zola sent an angry letter to the press, headed "*J'accuse*"—"I accuse"— which was published in January 1898. Zola was charged with libel. He was found guilty and given a one-year prison term. But before the sentence could be carried out, Zola fled to England. The next few months were miserable for him, since he spoke little English, and hated the food.

Zola returned to France in 1899, after Dreyfus had been pardoned. Even so, the political arguments raged on, and some people believe that an opponent of Dreyfus was responsible for the novelist's death. This occurred in 1902, when his chimney became blocked, and the fumes from a charcoal fire suffocated him. Zola was given a public funeral, and his remains were buried in the Panthéon, in Paris, an honor reserved for France's leading figures.

MAJOR WORKS

1867	THÉRÈSE RAQUIN
1871	THE FORTUNE OF THE ROUGONS (LA FORTUNE DES ROUGON)
1877	THE DRINK SHOP (L'ASSOMMOIR)
1885	GERMINAL
1887	THE EARTH (LA TERRE)
1889-90	THE HUMAN ANIMAL (LA BÊTE HUMAINE)

CLAUDE DEBUSSY

The influential composer Debussy rose from humble beginnings to lead the world of music in a new and exciting direction. His orchestral works are paintings in sound, appealing to the imagination as well as the ear.

Achille-Claude Debussy was born in a suburb of Paris on August 22, 1862, the first of five children. The family was poor, and the parents frequently ignored their children. Claude was often sent to Cannes to live with his aunt, Clémentine. She noticed the boy's attraction to music, and arranged his first piano lessons.

In 1871, Debussy's father, Manuel, met Antoinette-Flore Mauté. She recognized Claude's talent at the piano and declared that the boy must be trained as a concert pianist. She began preparing him for the entry exams of the Paris Conservatory of Music—the French capital's school for training musicians—which he passed in 1872.

For three years at the conservatory, Debussy made good progress. But, after failing to win first prize in a series of piano competitions, he gave up his ambitions to be a pianist, and turned to composing music. He began to experiment with new, controversial ideas that challenged existing musical beliefs.

Meanwhile, Debussy found a summer job as house musician to the millionaire, Madame Wilson-Pelouze. For the following three summers, he worked for a wealthy Russian patroness, Nadezhda von Meck, traveling throughout Europe with her family. Debussy loved the sophisticated lifestyle. He dedicated his first composition to Madame von Meck.

LIFE IN MONTMARTRE

Back in Paris, Debussy's studies progressed well, and he discovered a circle of like-minded artists and writers. He visited cabarets in the Montmartre district with the composer Erik Satie and the poet Raymond Bonheur.

Debussy also became friends with the beautiful Blanche-Adélaide Vasnier, a singer. He dedicated many of his songs from this period to Blanche. But

Portrait of Claude Debussy, 1903, by Jacques-Émile Blanche
This dark and atmospheric portrait shows the composer at the age of 31.

in 1884, their friendship came to an end when Debussy had to leave Paris for Italy. That year, he had won the conservatory's Prix de Rome. Part of his prize was four years of study in Rome.

Debussy disliked the Italian city, finding it "positively ugly." The only event that stirred him was meeting the aged Hungarian composer, Franz Liszt, who encouraged Debussy to seek out the Renaissance music—music dating from between the early 15th and 17th centuries—played in Rome's churches. Debussy found the music inspiring.

> "My music has no other aim than to … become identified with certain scenes or objects."
> (Claude Debussy)

After two years, he returned to Paris. On his return, he produced the major work required of him by the rules of the Prix de Rome, *The Blessed Damsel*. The Conservatory condemned the piece. The rejection did not worry Debussy, though. He had other problems—he was practically penniless.

NEW INFLUENCES

Nevertheless, he moved into a small Montmartre apartment, and began looking for wealthy patrons. He started to lead a cultured, bohemian—or uncon-

DEBUSSY AND THE HARP

Debussy broke conventions in his music. This involved giving new roles to instruments like the harp.

One of the oldest musical instruments, the harp (*right*) developed into one of the most popular solo instruments. As instrumental music became technically more sophisticated, so did the harp. It is now the only plucked stringed instrument commonly used in an orchestra. The strings are different colors: the C strings are colored red, and the F strings are blue.

Debussy is famous for rethinking the normal roles assigned to each section of the orchestra in order to allow him to create the exact sound he wanted. In doing this, he helped to elevate the role of the harp.

ventional—lifestyle, taking up the latest literary, artistic, and musical fashions. Somehow, he found the money to go to the Bavarian town of Bayreuth in 1888 and 1889 to see operas by the famous German composer, Richard Wagner.

The 1889 Paris World Exhibit exposed Debussy to an important new influence: Orientalism. He spent hours at the exhibit, listening to the rhythms

The rippling tones of the harp appealed to the Impressionists as an evocative instrument capable of creating atmosphere. Debussy used delicate harp scales to recreate the rippling motion of the waves, in *The Sea*, for example, and the gently shifting clouds in *Nocturnes*—a highly influential piece dating from 1899.

and tones of Far Eastern music, and especially Javanese gamelan music—an orchestra of gongs, bells, and drums. This influence affected much of his work for the next 20 years.

It was 1893 before Debussy produced his next work, *String Quartet in G Minor*. Critics were enthusiastic about the piece. One admirer called him "rotten with talent." The *Quartet* hardly

made him a household name, however, and he continued to live an aimless life.

Then, in 1894, his fortunes changed. Debussy produced a new composition, *Prelude to The Afternoon of a Faun*. This revolutionary piece, which critics claimed had no form, altered the course of French music, leading the way into the 20th century. The *Prelude* was a success all over Europe, and made Debussy's name.

MARRIAGE AND SUCCESS

By 1899, after many turbulent love affairs, Debussy had begun a relationship with a woman named Lily Texier. They were married in October that year. The composer also wrote the *Nocturnes* in 1899. It was first performed, to great acclaim, two years later.

The premiere of *Pelleas and Melisande*, in 1902, marked a turning point in Debussy's career. The piece was a new type of opera, in which the words were just as important as the music. It made Debussy the composer of the moment and the leader of a new school of music: "Debussyism." Yet he remained a private man, committed to his work, with no desire for public acclaim.

The opera's success brought the composer some financial independence. In 1903, he fell in love with Emma Bardac, a wealthy heiress. The two ran away together in 1904. His wife, Lily, tried to kill herself but lived, and began divorce proceedings. In 1905, Debussy and Bardac had a child, and they married three years later.

In 1905, Debussy premiered *The Sea*. The work was an immediate

Vaslav Nijinsky, 1912, by Léon Bakst
The famous Russian dancer Nijinsky danced the lead part at the première of Debussy's *Prelude to The Afternoon of a Faun*.

sensation, with critics comparing it with the Impressionist painting of artists such as Claude Monet (*see page 38*). Impressionist painters used color, light, and atmosphere to portray fleeting moments or to capture an impression of a subject. Debussy wanted to translate this effect into music.

To achieve this, Debussy reexamined the basic elements of music—melody, harmony, and rhythm—as the Impressionists had reexamined the elements of painting. He employed unusual "scales"—series of notes progressing up and down in order of pitch. He turned away from the traditional major and minor scales to ancient and Far Eastern scales. He approached harmony, too, in a new way. He often used chords which were traditionally regarded as

12

discords—jarring to the ear—claiming that they sounded beautiful. He also changed the roles of the different parts of the orchestra.

For two years after *The Sea*, Debussy produced little. But after his marriage in 1908, his creativity was astonishing, encompassing virtually every musical form. He also began conducting his own works. Although he was a poor conductor, and the concerts were agony for

---

"Strange, delicate, vibrating ... full of a deep ... poetry." (composer Paul Dukas on the *Nocturnes*)

---

him, the public flocked to see him, and the performances were a success.

In 1909, he was diagnosed as suffering from cancer of the rectum, but this had little effect on his musical output. He took drugs to suppress the pain, and he began to welcome commissions. Between 1909 and 1913, Debussy composed two books of piano pieces.

In 1911 and 1912, Debussy's revived creativity led to collaborations with two extraordinary personalities. The first was a Russian entertainment manager, Sergei Diaghilev, whose company— the Ballets Russes—was a great success in Paris. The project with Diaghilev, however—a dance set to *Prelude to The Afternoon of a Faun*—was a disaster that Debussy hated.

His other collaboration, with an Italian poet, Gabriele d'Annunzio, fared little better. Debussy wrote interludes for one of d'Annunzio's plays, but, again, it had a disastrous reception. Even *Games*, a ballet Debussy produced in 1912 after years of working with Diaghilev, failed to win acclaim.

FINAL WORKS

The outbreak of World War I, in August 1914, put a stop to Debussy's public engagements. In 1915, however, the composer wrote 12 *études*, or studies, his crowning pianistic achievement.

Although he was now very sick, he continued to pour out new works in a more severe style. He completed a trilogy—in three parts—*In Black and White*, for two pianos.

In December 1915, he had an operation, but the cancer was irreversible. Debussy spent 1916 recuperating and struggling to complete a violin sonata. This bittersweet work was his last. He finished it in 1917, and in January 1918, he was confined to bed. He died in his Paris apartment on March 25, during the last German bombardment of the city.

MAJOR WORKS

1887-89	THE BLESSED DAMSEL (LA DAMOISELLE ÉLUE)
1892-94	PRELUDE TO THE AFTERNOON OF A FAUN (PRÉLUDE À L'APRÈS MIDI D'UN FAUNE)
1899	NOCTURNES
1905	THE SEA (LA MER)

GLOSSARY

academic art A traditional way of painting based on the art of the past. Academic painters usually produced large-scale history paintings.

antique art The painting and sculpture of ancient Greece and Rome.

canvas A firm, closely woven cloth on which an artist paints a picture.

commission An order received by an artist, writer, or composer from a patron to produce a work of art, literature, or music.

composition The arrangement or organization of the various elements of a work of art, literature, or music.

Divisionism *see* Pointillism.

history painting A kind of painting that traditionally shows historical, religious, mythological, or literary subjects depicted in an impressive, noble manner.

impasto Thickly applied paint, usually oil or acrylic, on a canvas.

Impressionism The major movement in late-19th-century art. The Impressionists tried to capture the visual impression of a scene—particularly the changing effects of light—rather than its exact detail.

landscape A kind of painting showing a view of natural scenery, such as mountains or forests.

mythology A collection of stories about the gods or legendary heroes of a particular people.

naturalism A method in art or literature in which objects, places, or people are shown as they appear in nature or life, without idealization. Also Naturalism, a movement begun in the 19th century by Émile Zola. It attempted to show that ordinary human lives are determined by the laws of nature.

nocturne A short piece of music that evokes a nighttime atmosphere.

novel An invented story that is usually long and complex, and deals especially with human experience.

oil paint A technique developed in the 15th century in which colors, or pigments, are mixed with the slow-drying and flexible medium of oil.

opera A dramatic musical work, first developed in late-16th-century Italy, in which the characters sing the text, accompanied by an orchestra.

pastels Colored sticks made from a paste of white chalk and powdered pigment.

patron A person or organization that asks an artist, writer, or composer to create a work of art, literature, or music. Usually the patron pays for the work.

Pointillism A Postimpressionist painting technique in which dots of pure color are placed next to each other on the canvas. From a distance, the dots merge to create recognizable forms and a vibrant intensity of color and light. Also known as Divisionism.

portrait A drawing, painting, or sculpture that gives a likeness of a person and often provides an insight into his or her personality.

Postimpressionism A term describing the various artistic trends that developed in the late 19th century, especially in France, as a development of, or reaction to, Impressionism.

print A picture produced by pressing a piece of paper against a variety of inked surfaces, including engraved metal plates and wooden blocks. There are several different kinds of prints, including engravings, lithographs, and woodcuts.

quartet A musical piece usually composed for four string instruments or four singers.

realism The use in art and literature of subject matter drawn from everyday life and experience, rather than from historical, mythological, and religious subjects.

Renaissance The rebirth of classical ideas that began in 14th-century Italy, lasted into the 17th century, and led to a flowering of art and literature.

Salon The official, and most important, state art exhibit of France, held in the Louvre Museum in Paris.

scale A series of musical notes progressing up or down in order of pitch.

sketch A rough or quick version of a picture, often produced as a trial-run for a more finished work.

sonata An instrumental, as opposed to a vocal, piece of music.

still life A drawing or painting of objects that cannot move by themselves, such as fruit or flowers.

style The distinctive appearance of a particular artist, writer, or composer's work of art.

symbol An object that represents something else; for example, a dove commonly symbolizes peace.

Symbolism A movement developed in France in the late 19th century. The Symbolists expressed ideas, emotions, and moods through color and line.

technique The way an artist uses his or her materials.

FURTHER READING

Art in the Nineteenth Century, "Art & Artists" series. Thomson Learning, 1994

Bryant, Jennifer F. *Henri de Toulouse-Lautrec: The Artist Who Was Crippled*, "Great Achievers" series. Chelsea House, 1995

Greenfield, Howard. *Paul Gauguin*, "First Impressions" series. Abrams, 1993

Hunt, Lynn B. *An Artist Game Bag*. Derrydale Press, 1990

Janson, H.W. *The History of Art*. Abrams, 1995 (standard reference)

Janson, H.W. & Janson, Anthony F. *History of Art for Young People*. Abrams, 1992

Mason, Antony. *Cézanne*, "Famous Artists" series. Barron's Educational, 1994

Meyer, Susan E. *Edgar Degas*, "First Impressions" series. Abrams, 1994

The New Grove Dictionary of Music and Musicians. Grove's Dictionaries of Music, 1980 (standard reference)

Reyero, Carlos. *The Key to Art from Romanticism to Impressionism*, "Key to Art Books." Lerner Group, 1990

Ridley, Pauline. *Modern Art*, "Art & Artists" series. Thomson Learning, 1995

Thompson, W. *Claude Debussy*, "Composers World" series. Viking Children's, 1993

Wilkinson, Philip and Dineen, Jacqueline. *Art and Technology Through the Ages*, "Ideas that Changed the World" series. Chelsea House, 1994

Zola, Émile. *Nana*, "Airmont Classics" series. Airmont Publishing, 1970

INDEX

Picture Credits